PRAISE FOR *CO1*
GRANDCHILDREN

Don't let the title fool you. This is not some cutesy family collection of children's sayings and wise responses from grandparents. This is hard core reflections on faith and life. This is Theology 101, or maybe even 102. From Dr. Bill Tuck's mind and heart come words that have been seasoned from years of reading, thinking, praying, and being both pastor and Daddy. Tuck's underlying premise is that we, as we grow in age, so should our understanding of faith grow: "Clinging to childish notions of God when a person has matured in all other areas of his [her] life is to commit spiritual suicide." And fortunate for us, the questions are deep, the language is clear, and the answers are both deeply profound and simple. This book is for all of us.

Dr. Linda McKinnish Bridges, President
Baptist Theological Seminary at Richmond, Virginia

The Author of the faith taught that we must "become like children" and William P. Tuck provides the questions of children --his own grandchildren-- as a platform for teaching about life. Excellent for thoughtful adults. Scripturally-based and experience-rooted, Tuck's insights come from a lifetime of studying, preaching, teaching, guiding, pondering, and living.

Dr. Fred Anderson, Executive Director *Emeritus,*
Virginia Baptist Historical Society
and the Center for Baptist Heritage & Studies

This is a wise, mature reflection on many aspects of Christian faith and ethics, from a seasoned progressive Baptist pastor who knows what he is talking about. Highly recommended.

Rev. Dr. David P. Gushee
Distinguished University Professor of Christian Ethics
Director, Center for Theology & Public Life, Mercer University

Bill Tuck shares a unique and wonderful glimpse into conversations he has had with his grandchildren about life and how God is at the center of all of it. Bill reveals insights from his 40+ years of pastoring to simple yet penetrating questions about God and life. From questions about evolution, God's engagement in the world, to casual sex, Bill offers a perspective to some of life's perplexing questions about who God is and his expectations of us. This is a great resource for everyone—the seeking teen; the questioning collegiate; the equipping parent or grandparent.

Dr. David Olive, President, Bluefield College

Dr. Tuck has responded from his heart and his mind to questions his grandchildren have asked him. The questions are real and urgent ones, not pseudo-questions, and they concern ancient issues such as the suffering of innocent people and modern issues such as scientific naturalism. Dr. Tuck's answers are courageous, honest, clear, and respectful of the mystery of God. His objective is that readers will not only know about God but will know God in a personal way, and he accomplishes this by leading his readers beyond a childish to a mature faith.

Dr. Fisher Humphreys
Professor of Divinity, Emeritus, Samford University

Bill Tuck provides an invaluable resource for grandparents, parents, educators, pastors, who want to share the deepest values of our faith with our beloveds in the next generations. Offering wisdom from six decades as a pastor, seminary professor, community leader, husband, father and grandfather, Tuck addresses honest, probing questions of his grands—from pre-schoolers to college-aged and beyond—about such topics as the nature, images, and gender of God; the Jewishness, death, resurrection, and second coming of Jesus; and aging. Especially needed in this moment are helpful, age-appropriate reflections on the importance of science and its relation to faith. With nuggets like, "God inspires men and women, not books," Bill Tuck expresses profound insights in accessible ways.

Dr. Stephen Boyd
John Allen Easley Professor of the Study of Religions
Wake Forest University

William Powell Tuck, a native of Virginia, has served as a pastor in Virginia, Kentucky, North Carolina and Louisiana, and as a seminary professor, adjunct college professor and an intentional interim pastor. He is the author of 37 books including *The Journey to the Undiscovered Country: What's Beyond Death, Modern Shapers of Baptist Thought in America, The Church Under the Cross*, and *The Forgotten Beatitude: Worshiping Through Stewardship*. He was given an honorary Doctor of Divinity degree from the University of Richmond and in 1997 he received the "Pastor of the Year" award from the Academy of Parish Clergy. In 2016, he received the Wayne Oates Award from the Oates Institute in Louisville, Kentucky. He and his wife, Emily Campbell, are the parents of 2 children and 5 grandchildren and live in Midlothian Virginia.

OTHER BOOKS BY WILLIAM POWELL TUCK

Facing Grief and Death

The Struggle for Meaning (editor)

Knowing God: Religious Knowledge in the Theology of John Baillie

Our Baptist Tradition

Ministry: An Ecumenical Challenge (editor)

Getting Past the Pain

A Glorious Vision

The Bible as Our Guide for Spiritual Growth (editor)

Authentic Evangelism

The Lord's Prayer Today

The Way for All Seasons

Through the Eyes of a Child

Christmas Is for the Young…Whatever Their Age

Love as a Way of Living

The Compelling Faces of Jesus

The Left Behind Fantasy

The Ten Commandments: Their Meaning Today

Facing Life's Ups and Downs

The Church in Today's World

The Church Under the Cross

Modern Shapers of Baptist Thought in America

The Journey to the Undiscovered Country: What's Beyond Death?

A Pastor Preaching: Toward a Theology of the Proclaimed Word

The Pulpit Ministry of the Pastors of River Road Church, Baptist (editor)

The Last Words from the Cross

Lord, I Keep Getting a Busy Signal: Reaching for a Better Spiritual Connection

Overcoming Sermon Block: The Preacher's Workshop

A Revolutionary Gospel: Salvation in the Theology of Walter Rauschenbusch

Holidays, Holy Days, and Special Days

A Positive Word for Christian Lamenting: Funeral Homilies

The Forgotten Beatitude: Worshipping through Stewardship

Star Thrower: A Pastor's Handbook

A Pastoral Prophet: Sermons and Prayers of Wayne E. Oates (editor)

The Abiding Presence: Communion Meditations

Which Voice Will You Follow?

The Difficult Sayings of Jesus

Beginning and Ending a Pastorate

CONVERSATIONS
WITH MY
GRANDCHILDREN*

ABOUT GOD,
RELIGION,
AND LIFE

WILLIAM POWELL TUCK

Energion Publications
Gonzalez, Florida
2019

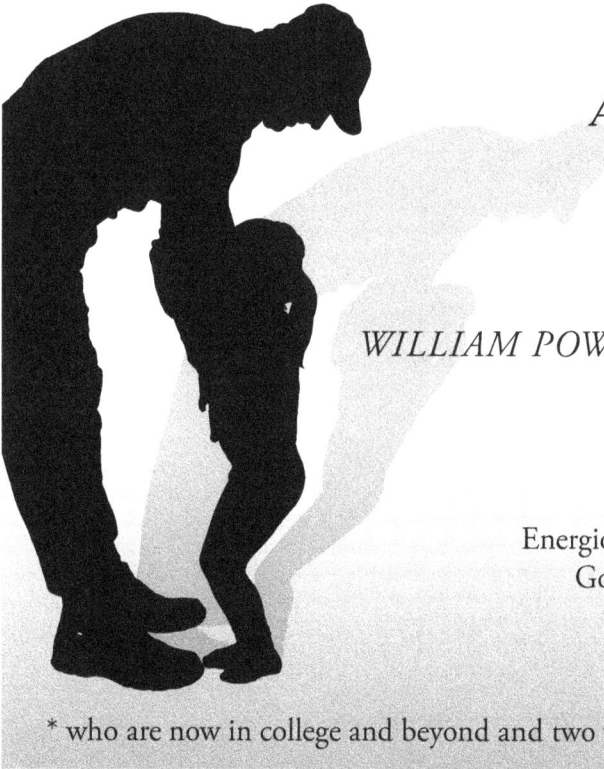

* who are now in college and beyond and two who are 4 & 8.

Cover Design: Henry Neufeld
Print ISBNs:
ISBN10: 1-63199-689-4
ISBN13: 978-1-63199-689-4
Library of Congress Control Number: 2019940514

Energion Publications
P. O. Box 841
Gonzalez, FL 32560
energionpubs.com
pubs@energion.com
850-525-3916

FOR

My grandchildren

J. T., Michael, Emily, Campbell, and Alden

May you grow deeper in your faith and understanding

of God's love

PREFACE

Few things in life can bring as much happiness as grand-children. Emily and I are fortunate to have two wonderful children and five delightful grandchildren. Three of our grandchildren are now young adults in college or beyond. Two are still small children, age four and eight at this writing. As grandchildren mature, they are confronted by many questions about life, God, religion, and other issues. I have served as pastor of several college churches and have heard many questions raised by these young people about God, the struggle to have faith, science and religion, sexual issues, the relevance or insignificance of the church, how to relate to friends or difficult people, and many other issues. The questions in this study reflect many of their questions along with my own grandchildren's inquiries. No one should claim to have all the answers to the many questions we encounter in life, and I certainly do not make such an assertion. My responses to the questions recorded in this book are simply my personal reflections, and I do not make any claim for giving the only authoritative answer to the many difficult questions we confront in our pilgrimage through life.

I am sure there are many other questions I have not addressed, but these are the ones that many young people are asking today. In my responses, I do not propose that I have given "the" definitive answer to all the questions raised. Whole books have been written on many of the questions the grandchildren asked. I have tried to offer a brief word, a theological point in a "nutshell," if you please, to point toward an answer, especially if one would inquire further in study and dialogue. I have added Scripture references to my answers in this printed version to guide the readers in having supportive biblical data.

I believe every parent, grandparent, and minister needs to be encouraging and open for young people to raise questions about religion and other issues and respond honestly without despairing comments about their questions. Be thankful that they care enough about religion even to have a question. My hope for this book is that it will serve as a guideline for young people, parents, grandparents, adult teachers, and ministers as a resource for addressing questions young people have about God and religion. As usual, I express my appreciation for proofreading the original manuscript, to my friend and fellow minister, Rand Forder, who himself is now a grand-father.

Dear Grandchildren:

I was pleased to learn that you were coming over this weekend. You indicated that you have some questions about religion and God. I can't wait to hear the questions. Join me in my library as we share together. We can sit and have an opportunity to reflect on your questions and concerns. Feel free to ask me whatever is on your mind.

Love,

Granddaddy

QUESTIONS ABOUT ...

Childish notions of God

Granddaddy: I'm so glad you have come. Did everyone get cookies who wanted some and a drink? Go ahead with your questions when you're ready!

Grandchild: As some of our friends have gotten older, they say they can no longer believe the teachings of the church. They say that they have outgrown these childish notions about God and the Bible. What should we say to them? Have we too outgrown these beliefs?

Granddaddy: Let me respond with a story first. Two men were seated next to each other on a plane and a neatly dressed young man turned his gaze from the window to the older passenger sitting beside him and introduced himself. Upon learning that his seat companion was a minister, the young man, who had stated that his occupation was an as-

1

tronomer, asked the minister if he would like to know his views on religion. Hesitating for a moment, the minister responded: "Well, sure."

The astronomer replied that all that a person needed to know about religion was the Golden Rule: "Do unto others as you would have them do unto you."

The minister was silent for a while, and then he asked the astronomer if he would like to hear his views on astronomy. With a puzzled look, the astronomer said "Yes."

"I think astronomy," the minister stated, "can be summed up in the phrase, 'Twinkle, twinkle, little star, how I wonder what you are.'"

So often men and women refuse to mature in their religious views and cling to childish notions of God and the divine purpose. Sometimes our views of God cannot stand the conflicts of the present age. When some have to discard certain childish notions of God, they feel that God also must be dismissed. That is like throwing the baby out with the bath water. If a Christian is going to grow to a mature faith, he or she must have an adequate view of God. Many factors influence our concept of God, and whenever one attempts to speak about God, he or she can speak only in terms with which one is familiar. Some immature views of God and religion should be discarded.

Grandchild: What are some of these childish ways we should discard?

Granddaddy: The way some people talk about God, it would seem that God is "a vague, oblong blur." The image appears so unclear in their minds that God is devoid of any real meaning or significance. Young people, at least some of them, say they believe in God, but when asked to tell what they think God's nature and activities are like, they are at a loss for words. Can it be true that many believe in "something" that is not clear or adequate for a sound faith? They have what I call a frosted glass view of God.

To many people, God is depicted as a sort of Santa Claus. Through the "frosted glass," God is seen as a sweet, nice, easy-going person who will reward us if we are good. In this picture, God is viewed as a "divine bellhop" who exists to serve us. Our wishes are turned into commands for God. Attention is directed toward the end of how God can serve us and not in how we can serve God. If this view is adequate to describe God, then the purpose of the cross of Christ is difficult to explain.

Sometimes God is depicted as a divine "grandfather" or "uncle" whose only thought is to make his children happy. God is pictured as being "old" and "remote," off in the "wild, blue yonder" far away from this world. His ways are also conceived as being "old-fashioned" and not in tune with the music of the day. The Bible that describes this God is read in an archaic language about people who lived centuries ago. The retired "grandfather" image leaves little room for a God who is contemporary and relevant to meet the needs of young people and adults today.

Many distorted images of God appear through the "frosted glass." God is a "venerable bookkeeper," who keeps the record of our behavior; a "policeman," who guides the conscience; a "living doll," whose purpose is to delight; "Uncle Sam," who gives protective freedom; and a divine "caretaker," who directs and controls the universe. These are a few of the inadequate ways God is seen when men and women seek to make God after the human pattern.

Grandchild: But we have heard some say that they are fearful of God and see him as judgmental.

Granddaddy: Yes. I have heard that too. In contrast to the view of God as "sweetness and light," some often think of God as a vengeful, vindictive, implacable type of demonic force demanding his "pound of flesh." To say that a person wills something to happen is to say that he *wants* it to happen. To assume that God deliberately sends suffering, broken bodies, cancer, accidents, and pain is to picture God as a "fiend." When God is depicted in this way a distorted concept of God's character is presented. A clear distinction needs to be maintained between God's "intentional will" and God's "circumstantial will"; what God intends and what God allows to happen. In giving us "free will," God opened the door for risks and abuses. In the New Testament, God has been revealed not as a God of vengeance, but as a God of sacrificial love.

Grandchild: Why do you think some have these views of God?

Granddaddy: For many, they draw these images of a "genocide" God from Old Testament passages like Deuteronomy 7, 1 Samuel 15 and Psalm 137: 9. We need to understand that the people then were primitive, and their concept of God is not on the level revealed in the life and teachings of Jesus of a God of unconditional love and grace. We have to realize that people grew gradually in their view of God, and we should not be trapped in a literal interpretation of Scripture that puts all passages on the same level. The teachings of Jesus and Paul always are more acceptable than some of the "childish" and immature views revealed in some of the Old Testament texts. To some, God is known only in a secondhand manner. Many young people have not had a firsthand personal experience with God. They have received their faith from their parents, accepted their friend's or minister's view of God, or married into a religion. Others have read about God, heard about God, sung about God, talked about God, but have not personally known God. Christianity by hearsay can never be adequate. No one wants to fall in love by proxy. Why settle for a secondhand faith? Genuine faith can exist only where there is conscious commitment to grow deeper in our knowledge of God.

Grandchild: How can we really have a mature faith? That doesn't seem easy in today's world.

Granddaddy: Let me respond with several examples. When a child of nine had a temper tantrum in a store, the exasperated mother cried: "Oh, don't be a baby!" The father of a teenage girl lost his temper over some trivial matter, and she had to calm him down by saying, "Daddy, act your age." Growing up is a part of life. Children grow mentally and physically. When physical growth is stunted by some tragic disease or accident, it is always sad. When a child continues to grow physically but ceases to grow mentally, the situation is even more disheartening. Just as the human body and mind were meant for growth, we all need to continue to grow spiritually.

In the little book, *Children's Letters to God*, it is humorous and even understandable when a small child writes God to send her a horse. She notes that she's kept her promises but still God has not sent her a horse. What's God going to do about it? But if the only prayer a young person can pray is, "Now I lay me down to sleep ..." his or her life indicates spiritual malnutrition. Failing to grow to a mature Christian faith is the primary cause of an improper concept of God. As the apostle Paul said, "When I became a man, I put away childish things" (1 Corinthians 13: 11). This includes putting away childish images of God.

Some young people and adults dismiss Christianity as "kids' stuff." It was all right for them when they were children, but now that they have grown up, they feel that they have "outgrown the religion bit." They have matured physically and mentally, but when it comes to talking about God, they use the same language and concepts that they learned in the church nursery. Just because someone clings to a particular childish idea of God does not mean that the Christian faith itself is childish. The Christian faith is a commitment to a continuously growing life in Christ.

Often the attention of the church is focused on individuals, but it is only to confront them with the need for salvation. They are then baptized and forgotten. Many Christians are like the man E. Stanley Jones said stood up in a meeting and remarked: "Twenty years ago, my cup was filled, and since that time nary a drop has gone into it and nary a drop has come out of it." Another said: "Then by this time there must be wiggle-tails in it." And there were! When growth ceases, a person's life becomes stagnant. The "new birth" in Christ marks the beginning of the Christian's life -- not the end of it. The spiritual growth of the Christian will have its ups and downs, but the Christian must never be content with his or her present growth. We will be constantly reaching toward perfection, striving to grow in maturity to be like our Master.

Knowing God

Grandchild: Can we ever fully know God or God's ways?

Granddaddy: In Rodgers and Hammerstein's musical, *The Flower Drum Song*, a song brightly presents the question: "How will we ever communicate without communication?" Here the Christian feels the thrust of this satire when we attempt to speak about God. To say that one can never look at the world from the divine perspective is not necessary, or is it? Several years ago, an interesting experience took place in one of our seminary classrooms. The professor had been giving his interpretation of a certain theological area, and when he paused for comment, one of the students declared quite sincerely: "Well, professor, we have listened to your interpretation, let's look at it now from God's viewpoint."

We simply can never know for certain what is God's perspective. Eternal truth is always read with misty eyes, or through a glass darkened by ignorance, superstition, or religious, economic, and cultural mores. We will always know less than we think, and yet more. We define faith in terms that are less than it is; and yet more than we understand. We stumble in trying to say what we mean, and yet we are keenly aware that our words conceal as much as they reveal. It is no wonder then why one must think of his or her faith in symbolical and paradoxical terms.

In the Bible, God is pictured as a shepherd, king, judge, father, brother, rock, fortress, and many other images drawn from human experience. Whenever a person attempts to speak about God, he or she does it with symbols, pictures, and familiar images. It is impossible to adequately describe God, but we speak in terms that we can understand. In the biblical record, God has been depicted in different ways by the writers. In each case men and women have tried to express in his or her own language the experience one has encountered with the eternal God. Our language cannot be exhausted or final in its description of God, but it can point others to the God who is seeking to make the divine presence known. The clearest image we have of God is the image that was focused in Jesus Christ. The New Testament bears witness to this image.

Grandchild: How would you describe God to an individual who does not believe in the biblical revelation?

Granddaddy: The questions that are often raised regarding God's revelation are: Why does God not declare himself more plainly? Why doesn't God give us a foolproof sign? Why doesn't God communicate with us in such a way that we can clearly understand God's message? What sign would we accept? Has not God already given us a clear, "unfrosted" image of himself in Jesus Christ? We cannot expect to receive more light from God if we have not responded to the light we have already received.

God can be described as truth, beauty, or goodness, but this sounds remote and abstract. No matter what symbol we use to describe God, God still remains out of focus until God is seen in a personal way. In Jesus Christ, the symbol is made real, the abstract becomes concrete, and the vague is rendered clear. In the person of Christ, we are able to see God in a clear focus. In Jesus Christ, the "very face of the Most High" has been revealed. Since each of us is a person, we can understand fully only that which is personal. The clearest image of God has come in the person of Christ. "God was in Christ, reconciling the world unto himself" (2 Corinthians 5: 19) is the event which places God in proper focus so we can comprehend the eternal nature of God.

Grandchild: How can we really know God?

Granddaddy: We do not have absolute certainty in our religious faith. The Christian faith is essentially trust. Trust is our complete reliance on God and the commitment of our self fully to God's guardianship. If a young person has heard the divine claim from God, then he or she must respond by obedience to that claim upon one's life. In responding to Philip's request to show him the Father, Jesus said: "He that has seen me has seen the Father" (John 14:9). We have received enough illumination about God through Jesus Christ to know what we have to do in life. If one yields his or her life in trust to the light revealed through Christ, although he or she may now "see through a mirror dimly," he or she has the clearest and most adequate image of the nature of God which one is able to grasp.

The difficulty of trying to understand what God is like is made even harder by these improper concepts. Most people do not worship a God that is big enough to meet the needs of their mature lives. Clinging to childish notions of God when a person has matured in all other areas of his or her life is to commit spiritual suicide. It is necessary for the Christian to continue his or her spiritual growth if one is to achieve spiritual maturity. Worship, study, prayer, fellowship, service, and a constant seeking to live in cooperation with God contribute to the Christian's growth.

Since we can describe God only in symbolic terms, our language is always limited in its description of God. But in Jesus Christ, the clearest image of God that our mind can understand has been unveiled. The Scriptures bear witness to this event. (You might want to look at John 14:9 and 2 Corinthians 5:19.) God can speak to us in many ways. God may communicate with us during corporate worship; while we work, study, or relax. Whenever and wherever the divine light comes to us, it issues an invitation that calls us to a life of discipleship and spiritual growth. It is a call to walk in the "company of the committed" and to participate in the abundant life.

Grandchild: Why do you think people try to know if there is a God?

Granddaddy: I believe that the desire to know God is a universal quest. We are incurably religious, and the urge to know God is an impulse planted by the Creator. Centuries ago the Christian writer, Augustine, expressed this feeling: "Thou hast made us for Thyself and the heart of man is restless until it finds its rest in Thee." "Show me how I can find God and I will believe," says the young man. Many, both young and old, have said the same thing. Throughout history persons have tried to find God, to see God, and to know God. But for some they have been searching without finding. They ask questions like: Is God at home? Is there anybody out there who understands and cares? Is God real? For centuries, philosophers and theologians have attempted to answer questions about the existence of God. Some have peered into the darkness and have seen only an inky blackness, while others have seen a radiance. Others have listened in the stillness and have heard only silence, whereas some have sensed the presence of God. What kind of evidence will convince men and women that God exists?

We need to remember that many of the greatest forces in the world cannot be seen with the naked eye. This does not mean that they do not exist or cannot be known. The force of gravity binds us to the earth with its laws. Electrical power lines give evidence of a concealed force. Words, sounds, and pictures can be conveyed to us on our computers, smart phones and iPads over "paths" we cannot see. The existence of God can be just as real, though God's presence may not be seen with physical eyes or touched by human hands.

 *Proving God Exists*

Grandchild: Can we really prove that God exists? I had a friend who took some philosophy courses in college that he said "proved" the existence of God. Can that be true?

Granddaddy: The attempt to prove the existence of God goes back more than two thousand years to the Greek philosopher, Plato. Since Plato's day, and especially during the Middle Ages, the "proofs" for the existence of God have been developed and interpreted. The philosophical arguments are based on something that is assumed to be true in an attempt to explain certain known facts. There are four principal philosophical arguments for the existence of God. Let me share each of the arguments briefly.

The first one might ask the question: How did this world get here? That's the *argument from design*. Take for example this illustration. Quite by chance, John found a box of old toys in his basement. As he examined them he noticed a well-constructed model airplane. The plane had been designed and built to the last detail. Not having seen the plane before, he thought to himself: I wonder who made this airplane? The workmanship is carefully done, and all the parts function well. Someone had to make it, or it would not exist. Arguments similar to this one have been constructed to try to "prove" God's existence.

This is called the *teleological argument*. This "proof" attempts to show God's reality from the apparent design or purpose of the universe. An English theologian, William Paley, (1743-1805) used a watch as his analogy to infer an intelligent Maker. Plato, Aristotle, and others have observed the wonder of the human body and the evident order of the natural world to demonstrate their case for God's existence. Those who· hold to this argument declare that design is seen throughout all the universe and, therefore, one must conclude that there is a "Designer."

The second "proof" might be called a thinking person's God. This is the argument from definition. Saint Anselm, an eleventh-century Christian, attempted to give one single argument that would be entirely sufficient to prove that God exists. Since then, other philosophers, including Bonaventure, Spinoza, Descartes, and Hegel, have proposed what is called the *ontological argument* for God's existence. Anselm stated that God is by definition "a being than which nothing greater can be conceived." But Anselm was quick to realize that it is one thing for an object to be in the mind, and another to understand that the object exists. He solved the dilemma, at least to his own satisfaction, by stating that God must exist both in reality and as an idea. By definition, God is that being which nothing greater can be conceived.

A third "proof" might be called what makes the world "tick"? This is the argument from cause. If a house burns down, the fire department will try to discover the cause of the fire. If the electrical power of a city fails, an investigation will be undertaken to determine the cause. From the time a child is old enough to talk, he or she wants to know the "why" of everything. The *cosmological argument*, then, could probably be correctly called the common sense "proof." It is the attempt to demonstrate the "why" of the universe. The logical argument is often put this way: Every event has a cause; the universe is an event; therefore the universe has a cause.

In looking for the reason why something "ticks," one must look beyond the thing itself. Our existence is dependent upon our parents' existence, and their life upon their parents', and so on. Every effect has· a cause, and that cause is the effect of something else which caused it. The proponents of this view argue that there must be some ultimate or first cause that is not itself caused. God is the first cause, they assume, that brought the chain of causes and effects into existence.

The last one I will mention might ask: What makes people act that way? This is called the argument from moral duty. The *moral argument* for God's existence was stated most forcefully by the eighteenth-century scholar, Immanuel Kant (1724-1804). Kant did not believe that men or women could prove God's existence by pure reason. He held that in the will or "practical reason," humanity was aware of an inescapable sense of moral duty. It is morally necessary to believe in God, Kant says, for without God men and women are unable to explain their sense of duty. According to this argument, man or woman's awareness of the difference between right and wrong and the obligation one senses to do what is right, can be explained only by the presence and demand of God upon a person's life.

Grandchild: Gosh. They sound very convincing. Do they really prove God's existence?

Granddaddy: To me they are proving without convincing. As convincing as the "proofs" for God's existence may sound, none of them is completely satisfying. It is very doubtful that a person who is personally devoid of any religious desires or convictions could be convinced that God exists. Trying to prove God's existence to those who are not already aware of God's presence is like attempting to teach a deaf man the difference between harmony and discord, or a blind woman the distinction between blue and green. The proofs may have meaning to those who are already aware of God's reality, but to those outside the household of faith, they sound flat and ring hollow.

Every philosophical proof for God's existence can be disproved by its opposite. Each proof is based on certain premises which reason itself is unable to prove. The famous lines from the French philosopher Pascal, state this feeling: "The heart has its reasons which reason knows nothing of." None of the "proofs" can bear the weight of a thorough examination. Let me mention the way the traditional proofs have been slain.

The *argument from design* runs headlong into a conflict with the Darwin position which points out the apparent useless waste in our universe, as well as the purposeful design. The problems of evil and suffering raise real questions concerning the design and purpose of the natural world. But the greatest weakness in the "proof" is that it does not prove what kind of God designed the world. This argument does not demonstrate that the "designer" is the type of God that would be worthy of worship. The *argument from cause* has a similar weakness. Suppose that a "first cause" or an "unmoved mover" is accepted, as being realistic, it does not necessarily imply that the "first cause" is a God who loves or cares.

The opponents of the *argument by definition* seek to show that existence is not the kind of quality that can be a part of the definition of any concept. The philosopher Kant argued that a person can think about having money but a hundred dollars in a person's mind is not the same as a hundred dollars in his pocket. It seems correct to state that if a person is to think of God, he or she must think of a God who exists. But it does not follow from this line of thinking, that what is necessary to make one's thinking consistent must exist outside one's own thoughts about it. Thinking about something in a certain way does not make it true or real.

The *moral argument* for God can be explained away by those who refuse to believe that the moral decisions men and women make are dependent on God. Some claim that our behavior is controlled only by social sanctions and our own acquired habits. The many cruel, coarse deeds of some men and women indicate to many that moral responsibility can be twisted to suit one's own purpose.

It seems doubtful, therefore, that there is any kind of argument that can prove the existence of God to a mind prepared to deny that existence. At best, the arguments for the existence of God are not "proofs" at all but serve only as pointers to help those who are already committed to God. Belief in God is not based on the conclusions of· arguments, but combined with the Christian experience, these arguments may give some clarity to the struggle to know God.

Grandchild: Is there any way then we can possibly know God?

Granddaddy: I believe that the only real way we can ever know God is through a personal commitment to the God we know through Christ. Knowing something about a famous baseball player is not the same thing as knowing him personally. A person might know how tall he is, how many years he played for, say, the New York Yankees, how many hits he made, and so on, but he still might not know him. To know a person is to be personally acquainted with him. The Old Testament uses the phrase "to know" God in this same sense. Where the Christians might use "faith" and "believe," the Old Testament speaks of men and women "knowing" God in a direct, personal encounter (Jeremiah 31:34). The New Testament writers present a similar emphasis in which the knowledge of God and faith are almost synonymous (Read, for example, Matthew 11:27; John 1:14; 14:10; Acts 2:36). Our knowledge of God is the personal communion into which God calls us by knowing God in Jesus Christ. The biblical revelation stands in contrast to the tradition which seeks to establish God's existence by "proofs." It calls men and women to a direct revelation of God. Jesus said: "He that has seen me has seen the Father; and how do you say then, 'Show us the Father?'" (John 14:9).

The best indication in the Scriptures of the personal aspect of God's revelation is in the Gospel of John where the author speaks of the Incarnate Word. The Word is not an impersonal term used to describe God's revelation but is an expression that is used to convey the fact that a personal manifestation of God was revealed when "the Word was made flesh" in the form of a specific man, Jesus Christ. The concept of the personal nature of God's self-disclosure is seen clearly in scriptures like John 1:1-16; 5:39- 40; Colossians 1:12-20; Philippians 2:5-11; and Hebrews 1:1-4. Knowledge of God is not derived from "proofs" about God or by accepting some ideas or propositions about God to be true. The awareness of God's reality is found in one's direct, personal encounter with God in the person of Jesus Christ (1 John 1:1-3; Acts 9:27).

Men and women are incurably religious and desire to know God. In their search for God, men and women have attempted to prove the existence of God by philosophical arguments based on our own powers of reason. At best, the "proofs" for God's existence can only serve as pointers and cannot be completely satisfying. The biblical writers do not attempt to prove God's existence, but confess out of their own religious experience. This experience is based upon direct encounter with God and is not built on secondhand inferences about him.

In any study of God, we need to realize that we are like a small child trying to see what is on the other side of a fence by peeping through a knothole. He cannot see everything because his vision is limited. But he keeps his eye fixed on the field of vision before him. The person who is seeking God does not have all the light, nevertheless, he or she follows the light that one is able to see and awaits further light. In moving forth in faith, each of us meets the God who is already seeking us.

God as Creator

Grandchild: A class-mate of mine, named Jim, and I are taking a biology class at State University and our professor had a lecture on "God, the Creator in a Scientific World." Jim thought that Professor Black's lecture seemed to take all meaning out of the biblical account of creation. He said that a person couldn't believe that and be a Christian and still believe in the Bible. It just isn't possible, he exclaimed! The professor said that the biblical creation accounts represented one of eighty-seven different creation accounts and bore the reflection of primitive man's thinking about the beginning of things.

Granddaddy : I think we should be careful in saying that a person is not Christian and that he does not think the Bible is trustworthy simply because a person interprets it differently. The Christian faith is a commitment to a Person, not to some ideas or propositions about God. To me the Scriptures are a record of the unfolding drama of God's acts, and God's revelation of himself in history--not just a compilation of propositions or concepts to which we are expected to give intellectual assent. God has revealed himself in the mighty acts of salvation, and the Scriptures are the literary vehicle that bear witness to the divine action. The method of the writers of the Genesis creation accounts wasn't historical writing; they wanted to confess through symbolic, mythological, or parabolic accounts humanity's absolute dependence upon God. You indicated that Professor Black said that the creation accounts used ancient literary forms and weren't intended as a scientific description of the physical details of creation. The use of figurative and symbolic language within the Scriptures, I believe, doesn't nullify the truth and meaning conveyed, however.

Grandchild: But Jim argued that the Bible tells us that God created the world in six days, then rested. "This ends the matter for me," he said. He asserts that the biblical account of creation makes any theory of evolution impossible; and that God created the world in six, twenty-four-hour days and rested on the seventh day.

Granddaddy: But why must the biblical accounts be read as historical narrative or as scientific explanation? The accounts obviously weren't written by eyewitnesses but by men who later were known by and knew God within history. They were trying to show, I think, in a mythological or parabolic way not how the world began, but that God is the Creator and that all of creation is utterly dependent upon and responsible to God. When you take the accounts as historical narrative, you turn God into a cosmic magician who snapped his fingers and said "hocus-pocus" or "abracadabra" and everything was created.

A view similar to that has been expressed by the poet James Weldon Johnson in his poem "The Creation." God is pictured anthropomorphically as stepping out on space, walking around, looking around, sitting down thinking, and talking aloud. Now everyone knows that this poem is to be taken metaphorically. It is very child-like in its expression about God and the creation;

nevertheless, Johnson's poem is a beautifully expressive picture of God as the Creator.

The biblical account, it seems to me is much like this poem. God is spoken of in beautiful but simple anthropomorphic terms; which means the writer thinks of God in human terms. God is depicted as speaking, and creation takes place at his spoken word. He walked in the cool of the Garden of Eden, and after creation he rested as if he was tired after a week's hard work. Surely God does not have vocal cords or legs. And if he can get tired from a week's work, how can he take care of a universe for all eternity? The creation accounts relate in childlike simplicity a reverent account of creation. They are not seeking to give a historical account of "the beginning" but are striving to stir within men and women an awareness of their own dependence upon God as the source of all life.

Grandchild: Jim argues that if God revealed the truth of creation to someone later, no one would have to have been there at the actual beginning to have recorded it. God could have revealed it centuries later to his writer and inspired him to record it so people would always know just how it happened. He believes that the Bible seems to stand in opposition to evolution and any other theory that denies the inspiration of the Scriptures. "The creation account is in the Bible and that is good enough for me!" Jim asserted.

Granddaddy: It is my understanding that there are at least two accounts of creation in the first two chapters of Genesis. They use a different style and language, and there is a variation in the order of events. I just finished a study of this recently. One creation story is found in Genesis 1:1 to 2:4a. This account shows an orderly progression of creation. It reflects a high concept of God: God created the heavens, earth, man, and the Sabbath by his mighty word. The other story is recorded in Genesis 2:4b-25. This account is much simpler and more primitive than the other. It is much more vivid and anthropomorphic, for it depicts God as breathing, planting, building, and molding. In Genesis 1:1 to 2:4a creation follows a planned design that begins with light and concludes with the creation of man. The story in the second chapter of Genesis begins with the creation of man and ends with the creation of woman. But these variations in sequence do not mean that the accounts are irreconcilable. It seems to me that each account makes a unique contribution, that each expresses one facet of the creation faith of Israel. The two accounts seem to be an attempt to give a fuller explanation of one central fact: God is Creator. They are not in conflict with each other but complement each other and enrich one central truth.

That is the significant thing about seeing God in these two creation accounts. God is depicted as sovereign Lord in both. God made the world and humankind, and God will have dominion over all of God's creation. The Genesis accounts can never grow old. They are independent of a day or an hour because they were written for all ages. By expressing the creation accounts in parabolic and mythological form, the writers have not limited the stories to the scientific view of any age. These accounts were probably transmitted orally from generation to generation before they were written down. When the writers finally recorded them as we have them today, the inspiration that guided the authors did not impress them with the scientific conceptions of the twentieth century. Modern science would have had no meaning to the people of that age. But the writers used the world view of their own day to convey a truth that isn't bound by any science. They used familiar pictures to show the revelation of the sovereign God within history.

Grandchild: Some of my friends argue that we should take the Bible at face value.

Science and the Bible

Granddaddy: Shakespeare described the forest of Arden as having "tongues in trees, books in the running brooks, sermons in stones, and good in everything." The literal-minded person would say that this is nonsense. Through symbolic words, Shakespeare conveyed insights that are not factually true. No one will argue that the parables of Jesus must all be taken as historical narratives to understand the message which Jesus was trying to express. When he said: "I am the light of the world," "I am the door," "I am the vine," or, "I am the good shepherd," Jesus was speaking metaphorically. The story of the prodigal son may have been the story of a particular man but is probably not a historical account but a parable of Everyman. The parable calls us to look into the mirror and see ourselves. Parables are not limited by science or age but are ageless in the message they seek to bear. This is to say, I believe, that God inspires men and women, not books, and is present in the written words because God was in the mind and heart of the writer. The written words, then, become a witness to the revelation. The words that are used are symbolic and may vary in meaning according to the cultural milieu and experience of humanity. Hence the words must be interpreted and reinterpreted to have meaning for each age. God is Creator and Redeemer whether the world is conceived scientifically as flat, square, or round. It is not necessary to accept the cosmology of the Genesis writers in order to acknowledge God as Lord and Creator.

Grandchild: Jim says that he cannot believe that the world came into existence through some accident billions of year ago. He says he will stick to the account of creation as it is written in Genesis to explain "how" the world began. What do you think?

Granddaddy: What else can you say to convince him? His position toward the interpretation of the Bible is an example of the very thing that has often caused conflict between science and religion. When a person says that one must take the scientific view of the Scriptures as well as its religious message, he or she is forcing many to "throw the baby out with the bathwater." They say: "Well, if I must believe that the earth is flat, has four corners, and came into being in six, twenty-four-hour days in order to believe in divine creation, then 1 must reject the religious viewpoint of the Bible as well as its scientific perspective." This is an attempt to force any thinking person to put his or her mind in a "straitjacket" and ignore many of the most obvious facts of science. I do not hear you telling me to forget about the development of the airplane, telephone, television, cell phones, the computer, smart phones, or modern homes with oil and gas heating--because the Bible doesn't mention them. Say what you please, but science is convincing. Who is going to deny the atomic theories after Nagasaki and Hiroshima? Nobody can put one's head in the sand and refuse to face the issue. Now, as I see it, if there is any conflict between science and religion, it will not be solved by reconciling the Genesis account with some theory of evolution. Our position as Christians today is not to defend a particular prescientific or scientific view of the world, but to communicate the religious message of the Bible.

Grandchild: Jim says that he is aware of the great advances of science, and accepts them and benefits from them. He acknowledges that we have witnessed many changes in the way we dress, the type of homes we live in, the way we travel, computers, Smart-phones, etc. He says that he is not against them and certainly wouldn't want to live in a tent when he can live in a warm house. But he asserts that he does not believe that science is an absolute authority and beyond criticism. He says that Anthony Standen has pointed out that the theory of evolution is one of the great generalizations of science. And that science is unable to test its theory by experiment, and scientists discuss this theory with a mass of overwhelming vague evidence which points to the similarities in life forms. When they say that all forms of life today have come about by a series of natural selections and changes, he states, they lose him. He boldly asks: "Where does God fit into such a scheme?"

Granddaddy: To say that the world came into being as an accident is to move from the realm of science to that of religion. Science has no more right to give answers in the field of religion than religion has to dictate scientific views. What science says about the process of evolution can be accepted as true, as long as one acknowledges that God is the purpose and power that activates the process. Scientists cannot give as a scientific answer that the evolutionary process just happened by chance. Science is based on the foundation that everything has a cause. Chance can't be taken as a valid scientific conclusion. Theistic evolution, which sees God as the purposeful cause of the evolutionary process, can be held, and is held, by many theologians as well as scientists.

Grandchild: Jim says he believes that I have just accepted this science bit, hook, line, and sinker. He asked me if I knew which was more important, science or God? If God is the most important thing in the world to us, and his way as Creator has been revealed within the Scriptures, he stated, then he chose to stand on God's side and not that of science.

Granddaddy: But I don't believe that it is that simple. I, too, believe that the Scriptures bear witness to God as Creator and sovereign Lord. However, I do not have to accept the Genesis accounts as objective historical narrative in order to do this. The writers were expressing in symbolic language an eternal insight about God's nature: God is Creator. Nevertheless, it is not necessary for me to accept as normative or final the conceptual images with which they express this truth. The scientific images and views may change from one generation to the next, but God remains Creator. Just because we no longer tend sheep in our town does not mean that God is not the Good Shepherd. We may have to use a different image now to express this truth, such as Comforter, Guide, or Director. In his book *God Is for Real, Man*, Carl F. Burke has related the way some young people in the tough part of an inner city have pictured God. Some of the spiritual truths are formed in ways that may seem novel or repulsive to some, but they have meaning to those teen-agers. The Shepherd of the twenty-third Psalm is vivid: "The Lord is like my Probation Officer." They use phrases like "God is Mr. Big" or the good Samaritan is a "real cool square." The Pharisee and the tax collector are called "The Wheel and the Character." To some this will be heretical and offensive, but to these folks, it makes God and the Bible real. They are still speaking about the same Bible and the same God, but in a language and way that is understandable to them.

Grandchild: Do the theological motifs of God as both Creator and Redeemer conflict with the scientific views of evolution and the origin of life? The central issue seems to focus on whether we can cling to our historical understanding of the Christian faith in a scientific age. A satisfying answer must take into careful consideration the impact, conflict, and relation between contemporary science and the biblical revelation of God as maker of heaven and earth. How do we respond to that question?

Granddaddy: The biggest stumbling block for most young people who attempt to study the Genesis creation story, I believe, is literalism. The unfolding drama of the creation accounts is often treated as if the events of that drama had been accessible to moment-by-moment photography. This, of course, was not the case. There were no eyewitnesses, no smart-phone cameras, no instamatic replays. Creation was God's act "in the beginning." Israel made theological affirmations about divine creation only in light of the redemptive activity of God in history. That redemptive activity was preeminently experienced by Israel in the Exodus. The biblical writers' theological affirmations about creation are not concerned with the past as once-upon-a-time. Their purpose was to witness to the faith that God was at the beginning of history and will be at the consummation of history, as God continues to be with us at the present.

If the biblical accounts of creation are read as objective historical narrative, then God tires, walks, works with his hands, and God talks aloud to himself. However, when one realizes that the ancient writers were describing God in terms understandable to men and women of that age, the accounts take on an ageless quality. The biblical writers did not hesitate to modify the cosmological world view of their own day and use it as a vehicle to transport the faith affirmations of the covenant community. This should be clear, but it has not always been understood or applied. In order to be truly biblical, we should do for our day and age what the writers of the Bible did for their own generation. It is unfortunate for a young person to have to choose between what he is taught about science in school and what he or she is taught in church. The ancient prescientific view of the world is not essential to the real message of the Bible. What is imperative upon the community of faith is that the substance of the essential message be recast and reinterpreted in forms and symbols that are clear and meaningful today.

Grandchild: Can we prove that God created the world?

Granddaddy: The Genesis account opens with the sublime utterance: "In the beginning God created the heaven and the earth." There is no attempt to prove God's existence. This is presupposed. At the beginning of things as we know them, God was present. Nothing existed before God and everything came into existence by God's action. The Hebrew verb *hara'* ("create") in Genesis 1:1, 21, 27 is used in the Old Testament exclusively of God's creative activity. Creation is exclusively a divine work and is utterly beyond human possibilities. Humanity is absolutely dependent upon God who alone is sovereign over the universe. The creation cannot be understood properly, however, as an independent fact. The biblical writers were not concerned with the question: How did the world begin? Their concern was with the God of history. God was known as a redeeming God within the history of Israel prior to God being known as a creating God. Creation marked the beginning of history, and the God who made a covenant with God's people in history is the God who created the world and is the beginning of history.

Grandchild: Many today who look at our universe ask the question: Who's in Charge Here?

Granddaddy: Since the giant rocket carrying Russian cosmonaut Major Yuri Gagarin was projected from its launching pad, soared into outer space, and returned, several decades ago, Russia has not failed to speak of the supposedly deadly blow that this scientific achievement has dealt against religion.

Since that time, other cosmonauts have been lifted up from this earth and have circled the globe in outer space numerous times. After his flight into outer space, the Russian cosmonaut, Titov, observed that he had not seen any signs of God while he was whirling about the world.

Religion, like humankind, has been thrust into the space age. The space age is placing a demand upon us to reexamine the Christian faith in the light of modern science. Some are saying that the space age reveals no signs of God. Others are calling for a clearer image of God than the "man upstairs" or the God who is "up there or out there." The Bible and science have met in the center of the twentieth-century arena and have locked horns for combat. The question that arises from the struggle really is: Who's in charge here? Is this an either/or dilemma? Must we choose between evolution and divine creation? Surely, we can acknowledge the impact science has made upon the interpretation of the Bible, and then proceed to reinterpret the Bible in the light of this knowledge without dismissing the Scriptures as outdated.

Grandchild: Wasn't the Old Testament written many years ago before we understood science as we do today?

Granddaddy: Yes. That's a good insight. If the conflict between religion and science is to be faced honestly, we must begin with the acknowledgment that the prescientific world view of the Bible is vastly different from the modern scientific view. The biblical writers used the "scientific" concept of the world that was prevalent in their day as a means of declaring a theological conviction. The Bible assumes a three-story structure of the universe: heaven, earth, and underworld. In the ancient picture of the universe the earth is a flat surface furrowed by mountains and divided by lakes and rivers. Above the earth is the firmament, which dikes the heavenly ocean and supports the abode of the gods. The earth itself is supported by pillars which are sunk into the waters of the nether world, in the depths of which is Sheol. The sky, the upper floor of the universe, is a solid vault above which God has his royal court. The waters are held above the vault of heaven like a super celestial sea and pour through the windows of heaven to bring the rain. The sun, the moon, and the stars move between the vault of heaven and the earth to give light. The earth is the center of the universe and all is observed from that viewpoint.

In many beautiful prose and poetic passages, the biblical writers described the world as it appeared to their eyes. "The earth is the Lord's, and the fullness thereof; the world, and they that dwell therein. For he hath founded it upon the seas, and established it upon the floods" (Psalm 24:1-2). "God said, 'Let there be a firmament in the midst of the waters, and let it divide the waters from the waters. And God made the firmament, and divided the waters which were under the firmament from the waters which were above the firmament: and it was so'" (Genesis 1:6-8). In many other places in the Old Testament, references are clearly descriptive of the three-story universe: Genesis 7:11; Exodus 20:4; Job 26:5-11; Psalm 104:1-13; Jonah 2:7.

The problem is apparent. Do we have to accept the pre-scientific view of the universe in order to receive the Bible's religious message? The significant feature about the biblical record is that its essential message is the personal self-disclosure of God to God's people within history. In God's revelation, God comes as Redeemer. The Bible is the written record that contains the message of God's redemptive activity. The biblical writers were not attempting to write books of science but were striving to present through parabolic, mythological, and symbolic means deep religious insights. The purpose of the creation stories was not to write a textbook or science but to awaken humankind to its dependence upon God, the Creator, and to their responsibilities to God (Deuteronomy 26:5-10; Psalms 24:1-2; 74:12-17).

Grandchild: What do you think the writers of the Bible were trying to teach us about creation?

Granddaddy: I think that the first two chapters of Genesis and the other creation references in the Bible are not a record of a cut-and-dried history. The Bible does not have as its purpose a description of the "how" or "what" of creation. The biblical writers were concerned with "why" and "who": "why" there is a universe and life, and "who" *is* sovereign. Science seeks answers to "how" the universe evolved, or examines "what" is already in existence. Science can explain how atoms behave but not why. It can give a description of how two molecules of sodium and carbon combine, but it is unable to state why. Science can show that quinine destroys malaria germs, but it cannot say why. There is an ultimate door through which science cannot pass. The biblical writers attempted to answer the ultimate question, "Why?" In powerful and ageless imagery, the writers say that God is the author and creative power that made the world. When one moves from the "how" of creation to the "why," he or she has moved from a scientific question to a religious one. Modern science has no more basis for judging the truth of religious convictions than has religion for forcing prescientific concepts on modern science. "The Lord is my shepherd" is true whether the earth revolves around the sun or the sun around the earth (Jeremiah 27:5; Isaiah 43:1,7,15).

The central theme of Genesis 1-11 could be summed up by any child in the simple sentence: "God made the world." In this ancient story, the supreme question of "Why?" is answered in the Creator God. Many Christians accept the theory of evolution as an attempt to give a biological description of the development of life without experiencing conflict with the biblical understanding of creation. To them, a human being as a creature who has evolved through nature is also a child of God, who has created the evolutionary process that caused man and woman to advance. Men and women are not creatures of blind fate but the products of the eternal God who has used many "methods" to perform God's creative activity. The theory of evolution need not stand in contradiction to the Bible. The purpose of the Bible is not to trace the development of humankind from a single cell to contemporary man or woman. This is the realm of science. No matter what method of creation God used, the Bible declares that the origin of the whole universe, including humankind, has its source and *telos* in God (Psalm 104; Job 38:1-41).

*God's relationship
to creation and humanity*

Grandchild: I remember reading about a prospector or a settler during the close of the last century who had staked a claim for a piece of land or a gold mine and frequently had it stolen by a claim jumper. Often the matter was settled, so TV shows and movies lead us to believe, by a gunfight or a physical duel. The winner was then declared the owner. Do we not have a similar fight going on today about who owns the earth?

Granddaddy: You have a good insight and a good question. The struggle for ownership of land rights is much older and more universal than the last century, however. It is a conflict. that has been going on since men and women have been upon the face of earth. The experience of Adam and Eve is not just the story of one man and one woman; it is the experience of the struggle of Everyman and Everywoman to be masters of the earth and to be freed from God's dominion. It is the desire to own the earth as one's own, free from any claims. It is the desire to be a god. (Genesis 3:5)

Who owns the earth? Communists teach that it belongs to the workers. Socialists declare that the state is the owner. Capitalists claim that ownership belongs to those who can attain it by an uneven combination of their own intelligence, strength, and freedom. Without acknowledging a prior claim by God, every one of humanity's systems is a claim jumper. Who owns the earth? The psalmist has answered: "The earth is the Lord's, and the fullness thereof; the world, and they that dwell therein" (Psalm 24:1).

Genesis opens with two accounts of creation. In Genesis 1:1 to 2:4a man is created last; while in the Genesis 2:4b-25 account, man is made first. However, both stories teach that man, the crown of creation, is to have dominion over the rest of creation (Genesis 1:26-28; 2:7). Often man forgets, though, that he has only a delegated dominion. He is lord of creation only as he acts as a steward responsible to God who gave him this privilege. Man does not act for his own honor and glory; he is to serve as God's living image on earth. Man was created for "the glory of God" and not just for his own happiness (Isaiah 43:7). The one who has been created in God's "image" (*imago Dei)* is to be God's representative. Only humankind has the ability to have fellowship with God. He/she alone of all creation is the one who can respond to God in trust or rejection (Psalm 8:3-5). The Sabbath, the final climax of creation and the symbol of humanity's need for worship, depicts humankind's fellowship with God and is a foretaste of their eternal fellowship with God. Of all of God's creation, man/woman is the only one who can respond to God in worship (Exodus 20:11; Hebrews 4:1-11).

Grandchild: Does the New Testament give us any further light on this subject?

Granddaddy: Yes, I think it does. In Jesus Christ, God has revealed that God's eternal purpose is to have fellowship with his created man/woman. Humankind can become truly human only when they realize their complete dependence upon God and yield their life in obedience and faith to the Creator. In Jesus Christ, humanity has seen revealed the extent to which God has gone to restore fellowship and purpose in humankind's life (Hebrews 1:3). This same God has revealed through his Son that his inner nature is love (John 3:16). God as Creator was motivated by the same eternal love that was revealed in God's Son. The creating God has always been a redeeming God. The two concepts are intertwined and the concept of salvation is rooted in the idea of creation.

Only if God is Creator can God claim man/woman as God's own. Because God has created us, God can demand obedience, and only One who has made us for God's self can restore the broken fellowship. Having created humanity for fellowship, God alone has the right and the power to forgive and redeem us. Salvation is God's act to bring us "home again" into the fellowship for which we were created. Because God is the source and origin of all of creation, God is able to redeem us. Salvation is God's act to enable us to fulfil our true nature (Look at these Scriptures Ephesians 1:9-10; 1 Corinthians 8:6; Psalm 74:12-17; Isaiah 40:12- 31). Creation and redemption are inseparably related. Creation is not just a theory about the beginning of history: it is the first of God's saving acts that continued to unfold until the fullness of God's grace was made known in Jesus Christ.

Creation is understood in the New Testament in light of the revelation in Jesus Christ. In Christ, God has accomplished a "new creation" which completes and restores the broken relationship that sin has caused between God and his creatures. The original creation anticipated the new creation, and the new creation fulfils the divine beginning. Although the creature's rebellion hindered his fellowship with God, the divine creative intentions are fulfilled in the new creation (Ezekiel

36:26-28; Isaiah 40:12-13; Ephesians 1:9-10; 2 Corinthians 4:6; Romans 5:12-14 might be helpful here).

If we try to jump God's claim, then we only succeed in losing the very thing that God desires to give us freely. God has commanded humanity to "subdue the earth," but we must remember that we lose this privilege if we are not willing to acknowledge that we have received this honor from the Maker of heaven and earth.

Granddaddy: We have had a long discussion about this theme of creation. Let me offer a brief summary. I don't think that the conflict between science and religion needs to exist. The purpose of the Bible is not to teach a scientific view of creation but to make the theological affirmation that God is Creator. The Scriptures are not concerned with the "how" of creation but with the "who" and "why." The Scriptures seek to declare in a pictorial and symbolic manner that God is the source and power upon which all of the universe depends. God has the right to demand obedience since God is Creator. We can fulfil our nature only when we are in fellowship with God. Since we were created for fellowship, God is able to bring the redemption that can restore this fellowship which we lose in sin. Where God in Christ is actively engaged in our salvation, God is working creatively as God did in the beginning. Wherever God's redemptive activity is at work, that is nothing less than a "new creation."

Providence of God

Grandchild: In a folk song entitled "Old Coat," Peter, Paul, and Mary have voiced the feelings of frustration that many of us have today. I along with others wonder, "Is life a matter of fate, luck, chance, or fortune? Is the answer 'written in the wind'?" Can we say that "God's in his heaven and all's right with the world"?

Granddaddy: Obviously, all is not right with the world. The past few years have been a depressing record of violence and uncertainty. The hot and cold wars between East and West have raged incessantly. Poverty, terrorism, racial injustice, and the urban crisis have encountered head on the philosophy of "see no evil, hear no evil, speak no evil." The assassination of prominent American leaders and terrorist attacks around the world have left ugly scars in the body of the democratic way of life. Violence, murder, and anarchy have happened too often in our world.

Life is no bed of roses; to some people it is almost all thorns. From various quarters come pronouncements that we have now arrived in our culture to a time of the post-Christian age. Some writers are so bold as to declare that we are now living in a deserted universe--not only in a post-Christian era but in a post-God era. Our age has been described as the century of desertion. In Aldous Huxley's fantasy novel of the future, *Brave New World,* the Savage asks the World Controller of the Universe:

"Then you think there is no God?" The Controller answers: "No, I think there quite probably is one." The Savage then asks: "How does he manifest himself now?" "Well," the World Controller replies, "he manifests himself as an absence; as though he weren't there at all." In much of contemporary drama and literature there is an insistence on the absence of God in a world of violence, frustration, guilt, loneliness, and anxiety.

Grandchild: Has God, having created the world, deserted it? And is God now lounging in an eternity of rest and ease? Is God remote from this world, uncaring and uninvolved? Has he gone on vacation to a blissful celestial resort? How do we resolve the problem concerning God's control of the world in light of present world conditions? Is it possible that God can still be "creating"? How does God conserve and renew the world?

Granddaddy: Today many airplanes are equipped with a device called an automatic pilot. After the pilot has soared the plane into the sky and has headed it toward the destination, he can set the controls and turn on the automatic pilot, and the plane will maintain its assigned course. The pilot can then relax and let the automatic pilot control the plane. Sometimes this is the way God's creation is viewed: God created the world at a certain time in the past, then he set the course of the universe on automatic and sat back to rest. To some the universe is like a clock that, since it has been made by the perfect clockmaker and set running, does not need ever to be rewound. It continues to run automatically. Advocates of this view depict the world as a self-winding system. Deism, as this position is called, pictures God as the Great Architect who, having created the universe as a smooth-running machine, takes no interest in it and does not care for it. God remains aloof from his handiwork and does not "tinker" with it. But is that the way it really is?

I heard about a college student who told his professor that he believed that the universe was nothing but a vast machine which made, repaired, and ran itself. The professor asked the student: "Did you ever hear of a machine without a pedal for the foot, a lever for the hand or an outlet for connection with some outside power?" The student replied that he had not seen such a machine. "Then," said the instructor, "we had better not think seriously of the universe as a machine."

Often as one drives down a busy city street or along a main highway, he or she will see this sign: "Caution: Men at Work." Maybe this is the sign we need to have flashed occasionally into our minds about God. Everywhere signs seem to indicate, "Caution: God at Work." God has not taken a trip into the wild blue yonder and deserted his world to the forces of chance or to a self-repairing system. God is still at work in his world. God is at the controls of his universe. Creation is more than a Big Bang that happened once-upon-a-time. Creation is God's continuous act as he remains at work in his universe. Jesus voiced this truth when he said: "As my Father has continued working to this hour, so I work too" (John 5: 17, Moffatt).

Grandchild: How can we, as Christians, converse with those who are atheist?

Granddaddy: I think we have to begin in a friendly and open manner and not in an argumentative or accusatory tone. Our atheist friend may hold his or her view because of problems relating to questions about evolution, human suffering, natural disasters, the authoritarian attitude of some religious believers, scientific questions, or other issues. I personally can be sympathetic to many of these issues. Many of them are not easily answered. Remember the professor's comment about not viewing the universe as a machine that operates on its own without a source of power? This to me is a genuine issue for the atheist to confront. Can a person really believe that this universe with all its intimate details, the human body with its intricate mechanism, the vast order of the whole universe just happened by chance? That is a hard thing for me to believe. Did there not have to be some source, power, God, if you please, that designed and set it all in motion? That seems more likely to me than the notion that everything just came about by some vast chance. Did human beings of their own cognition become aware of the importance of moral and ethical behavior toward others? That seems also unlikely to me. I believe that to suggest that everything came about by mere coincidence is more farfetched than to suggest God as the resource. This is where I would begin the conversation.

Grandchild: Some of my friends argue that you can't believe in the Bible and science at the same time.

Granddaddy: No young person should be forced into an either/or decision: either God and the Bible *or* science. Today the issue is seldom creation versus science. The two have become allies, and many writers have discussed the relation between creation and science. Many theologians, and some scientists, now use the term "creative evolution" 'to explain God's continuous creative activity. This concept has found various expression: Henri Bergson spoke of "creative evolution," as did Emil Brunner; Lloyd Morgan's term was "emergent evolution"; Alfred North Whitehead used the phrase "principle of concretion." Kirtley F. Mather, Hendrikus Berkhof, Teilhard de Chardin, Paul Tillich, Eric Rust, and other religious writers have used similar categories to express the same truth.

Creation is not simply something that happened once-and-for-all but is in some way continuous. God's acti*vity* in sustaining the universe is usually referred to as the providence of God. Whether one refers to God's control of his world as creative evolution or providence, the significant truth in both terms is that God has not deserted his creation. God is still guiding, directing, and caring for it. The world is no more able to continue on its own without the sustaining power of God than it was able to come into existence on its own (See Colossians 1:17; Hebrews 1:3).

Grandchild: In what way is this possible?

Granddaddy: God is creating anew. God is creating in the movement of the planets and stars throughout the vastness of the universe. God is creating in the cycle of the seasons and in the newness of the flowers and grass. God is creating in the circulation of blood throughout the vascular system of our bodies. God is creating in the birth of each newborn child. God is creating anew in the works that come from the minds of men and women in poetry, music, art, scientific advances, religious insights, and in countless other ways. God is creating in the ability of the eye to pick up the words from a page and have them carried to our brains and produce thought and reflection. God is eternally creating and sustaining the world. At every moment, God is vitally concerned with his creation. "From him, and through him, to him, are all things" (Romans 11:36). (See also Psalms 104; 139; Philippians 2:13; Matthew 5:45; 6:26-34; Romans 8:21-28.)

Grandchild: Does this mean that God needs a vacation?

Granddaddy: Everybody needs a rest from work or a break from his or her studies. A trip to the beach. the mountains, the country, or some other favorite spot gives us relaxation, rest, play, and leisure. Every person needs to get away from it all occasionally and "let his hair down." Many students can tell you about the "dragged out" feeling they get when they have gone too long without sleep. Too many long hours on the job can quickly wear down a person unless she can find some opportunity for a quick nap or a few moments of rest. We readily admit that this is true concerning ourselves, but how about God? Does God need a rest, a nap, a snooze, or a vacation?

What a ridiculous question, we say. And we laugh at it until we read again the Genesis story of creation. "On the seventh day God ended his work which he had made; and he rested on the seventh day from all his work which he had made" (Genesis 2:2). Why did God rest after his creative work? Did the six days of work make him weary and tired? If God can become tired after a few days of work, how can God take care of a universe for an eternity? These are serious questions and cannot be answered lightly. If we realize, however, that the biblical writer was describing God in terms which would be familiar and understandable to his readers, the problem is not as acute. God is being depicted by the biblical writer in human terms, and the Creator's sabbath rest gives meaning to humanity's need for rest from work. Evidently the writer was seeking to show that the origin of the sabbath as a day of rest was found in the divine sanction. God hallowed this day and set it apart for rest (Genesis 2:1-4a; Exodus 20:11; 31:17; Deuteronomy 5:15).

Grandchild: I'm confused. How can we speak of God needing rest?

Granddaddy: The biblical word for rest does not mean having a rest or relaxing but refers to the idea of God's ceasing from God's work. It is the completion or accomplishment of God's divine activity. It is not the rest of a worn-out. tired, drowsy God, but it is the rest of the Creator. Even in divine rest God is the Creator. The Genesis writer is bold enough to write that God "finished his work" on the sabbath day before he "rested" (Genesis 2:1-3, RSV). God's providence must be at work at all times or the universe cannot be sustained (John 5:17). Even as a creating, working God, there is peace and rest at the center of God's being. God invites humankind to participate in divine restfulness, and the sabbath day has become the symbol of that eternal rest which God alone is able to provide.

Grandchild: Does this mean that God has left us alone or deserted us?

Granddaddy: The popular spiritual, "He's Got the Whole World in His Hands," has inspired millions with its great truth. stated so simply. The image of God's hands is symbolic of God's sustaining grace and care. The Christian lives with the assurance which was echoed long ago by an ancient writer: "The eternal God is thy refuge, and underneath are the everlasting arms" (Deuteronomy 33:27). God has not created the world and left the world to itself. God is still active in creation. The psalmists and the Old Testament prophets saw God's hand in the events of nature and history. Nothing was outside God's providence. Jesus spoke of God as the one who clothes the lilies of the field, feeds the birds of the air, sends the rain upon the just and the unjust, and knows the very number of hairs on a head.

Grandchild: "Does this concept of the providence of God hold up in the light of modern science and contemporary knowledge?"

Granddaddy: Often God's providence is described by some as a sort of divine insurance policy that God provides to give us good health. success, food, clothing, material and physical securities and to protect us from physical harm. This suggests that God plays favorites and is a sort of divine policeman who protects his own from all physical suffering or harm. Early Sunday morning on June 4, 1962, when your grandmother and I were living in Atlanta, Georgia, an Air France Jet crashed and burned in takeoff near Paris. All 132 passengers aboard were killed, except two airline hostesses who were thrown to safety when the tail section snapped off. Killed in this flaming crash were 122 civic and cultural leaders of Atlanta. The question that was on almost every lip was, Why? Why does God allow such things to happen? The world is full of crime, war, disease, poverty, hunger, calamity, terrorism, and sorrow. Where is God's providential care?

Does God's providential care mean that Christians are spared from suffering and pain and will have only the blessings of happiness and physical security? All anyone has to do is to look around him to realize that this is not true. Some of the most faithful saints have suffered years of intense agony, pain, and trouble. The church does not offer a magical escape from all pain and difficulties. According to Luke 21:8-19, Jesus said that the Christian might suffer wars, physical calamities, economic loss, and many other distresses. God "spared not his own Son, but delivered him up for us all" (Romans 8:32). God does not exempt Christians from suffering and difficulties but assures us of the divine Presence with us even in the midst of our suffering and difficulties.

Suffering and difficulties

Grandchild: Why does God allow suffering and difficulties?

Granddaddy: That's a good question. Maybe God knows that this is a way we learn and grow. Consider what some persons have accomplished under hardship and suffering. It is difficult to know what part suffering played in their spiritual growth. The important consideration seems to be man's or woman's interpretation of and reaction to what happens to him or her, not the event itself. John Milton wrote some of his greatest poetic works after he became blind. Beethoven composed some of his masterpieces after he became deaf. Louis Pasteur accomplished some of his most brilliant work after he suffered a paralytic stroke at the age of forty-six. Dostoevsky, the great Russian author, was an epileptic. The apostle Paul suffered from a "thorn in the flesh." He prayed for its removal, but God answered: "My grace is sufficient for thee: for my strength is made perfect in weakness" (2 Corinthians 12:9).

Grandchild: Do you believe that God protects Christians from troubles and suffering?

Granddaddy: God does not protect us from suffering and sin. God is the creative artist who, still at work in his world, can bring beauty and wholeness out of agony and wrong. The Scriptures do not teach that everything turns out all right, but "we know that in everything God works for good with those who love him" (Romans 8:28, RSV). An enduring truth of the Scriptures is not that God frees us from all problems and suffering but that God promises us that nothing can separate us from his love. (See Romans 8:38-39.) God's power enables us to have inner strength to confront the difficulties of life. When a storm strikes an eagle, he positions his wings in such a way that the very fury of the air currents sends him above the storm. The position of the wings does it. God has implanted "wings" in the heart of the Christian to guide us through the storms of life. We are not removed from the storms, but we are strengthened within to confront even the most violent storms. Nothing can separate us from the love of God when we are in Christ Jesus, our Lord.

God's ultimate will cannot be defeated by sin, ignorance, or natural calamities. The ultimate goal of our life is not found in material and pleasurable gains but in eternal qualities that can never be destroyed by external surroundings. God's providential care is the Christian's assurance that nothing can prevent us from fulfilling the ultimate meaning of our life. Faith gives to the Christian an inner security that enables him or her to meet all the circumstances of life.

The late Paul Tillich has summed up this position so clearly: "Providence means that there is a creative and saving possibility implied in every situation. which cannot be destroyed by any event. Providence means that the demonic and destructive forces within ourselves and our world can never have an unbreakable *grasp* upon us, and that the bond which connects us with the fulfilling love can never be disrupted."

I believe that when God created the world, God did not desert it. God's providential care has continued to sustain and direct it. How long it took God in his creative process is not the important consideration. What is important is that God is the Creator and that God *is* still active in his creation. The purpose of history is grounded in the fact that the One who created "in the beginning" will be "in the end God." He is "the first and the last" (Revelation 1:17). From beginning to end, the history of humanity and the universe is grounded in the sovereign God who has revealed himself in Christ as the "Alpha and Omega" (Look, for example, at Revelation 22:13; 1:17; 1 Corinthians 8:6; 15:24-28).

Time and Eternity

Grandchild: What does creation tell us about the relation between time and eternity? What is the relation between temporal life and eternal life?

Granddaddy: "Time marches on" and "time waits for no man" are familiar phrases. A theme song from one of Simon and Garfunkel's albums expresses the swiftness of the passing of time. A person can sing "the times, they are 'a-changin','" and we know what she means. But if she says that time itself has changed, this is a different matter. Everyone will admit that the world has changed considerably since the turn of the century. Other changes are also apparent. Night passes into day, day into night, summer into fall, fall into winter, and winter into spring. The changes continue endlessly. When someone wants to know the time, he can look at a clock or a watch. However, if he asks what time is, the answer is not easily given. Expressions about time fill our vocabulary. Almost every day we hear and speak about killing time, saving time, wasting time, no time like the present, time will tell, I haven't got time or time is money. Although many have engaged in conversation about time, few have taken the time to examine time. Hopefully, these few minutes will allow us to spend some time looking at time.

Grandchild: What do we mean when we speak about "Finding Time?" What is time?

Granddaddy: For most people, their only thought about time is getting up on time, catching the bus on time, and arriving at work or school on time. Time measured by the second, minute, or hour, and the position of the clock hands usually determines the day's activities. Our minds are accustomed to conceiving time as that which is measurable and uniform.

This was not the case, however with the biblical view of time. Time was not seen as an abstract frame in which events could be placed side by side. From the biblical viewpoint, the duration of time is not the significant factor. The biblical viewpoint is concerned with a definite point of time where a specific moment is decisive. The Bible does not speak of time in an impersonal sense; time belongs to God and serves God's purposes. Time, then, in the biblical sense, comes as an opportunity from God and is not something that we ourselves can determine. It comes as a summons to obedience.

Events that come to us present themselves as an "opportunity," but their fulfilment comes as man or woman responds to this opportunity. The writer of the book of Ecclesiastes stated this principle when he said: "To everything there is a season, and a time to every purpose under the heaven" (Ecclesiastes 3:1). In the Bible, time is seen as the opportunity God provides: in natural events (Psalm 104:27; Jeremiah 1:16; Ezra 10:13), in history (Psalm 11:15; Jeremiah 1:17-20), in birth and marriage (Genesis 38:27; 1 Samuel 18:9), in various other "times," some of which are listed in Ecclesiastes 3:1-8.

In the New Testament, the time toward which the prophets had looked arrived within history. At the beginning of his ministry, Jesus read a passage from Isaiah 61:1-2 in the synagogue at Nazareth and then declared: "This day is this scripture fulfilled in your ears" (Luke 4:21). In another place, he stated that "the time is fulfilled, and the kingdom of God is at hand" (Mark 1:15). "My time is at hand" (Matthew 26:18). God's opportunity is expressed within time and comes as a call to commitment which man can accept or reject. Jesus said that Jerusalem would be destroyed "'because you did not know the time of your visitation'" (Luke 19:44, RSV).

The moment of opportunity comes not in an abstract call to be good, kind, and honest to everybody. It comes in daily, sometimes hourly, encounters with people. The summons to service and obedience comes where we live in the concrete city in the struggle against poverty, ignorance, inequality, and war, in the halls at school, at work, on the bus, with the neighbor down the street, with the yardman, with the elevator operator, with the janitor, with the young girl whose mother has just died, with the boy or girl in trouble. The time of opportunity comes in many forms, masks, and shapes. We respond as we have eyes to see the time of God's summons.

Grandchild: Where did time come from?

Granddaddy: The Bible locates the origin of time in the creative act of God. God created time when God organized the days and seasons (Genesis 1; 8:22). In the beginning of his creation God initiated time (Genesis 1:1: John 1:1-2; Hebrews 1:10). God is thus the Lord of time, and God has established this order for the guidance of the universe and humankind. God is the creator, sustainer, and director (Jeremiah 33:20; Isaiah 49:8; Psalm 69:13). Since God is not in time, as a human being is, God is not limited by time as we are. The times and the seasons are in God's control (Acts 1:7; 1Timothy 2:6; Titus 1:3). Time is a function of God's own purpose, and one day will be absorbed into God's eternity (Psalm 90:4; Isaiah 60:19-20). Time for humanity appears to be moving in a straight line. A man or woman is able to see only a part of it at a time, but God is able to see all of it. God has no past or future; God is the ever-present Lord. God is the Eternal Lord for whom a thousand years or one day is all the same (2 Peter 3:8). God, not humanity's clocks or calendars, determines the true measure of time. "I am the first, and I am the last" (Isaiah 44:6). "Him who is and who was and who is to come" (Revelation1:4, RSV). God is not affected by the passing of time; God remains "the same yesterday and today and forever" (Hebrews 13:8, RSV).

The Western system of determining time from the birth of Christ originated in the eighteenth century. Once this was done, our calendars themselves indicated that the coming of Christ forms the center of history. The Christ event marks the "mid-point" of history where God reveals he has time for us. This unique entrance can be designated by dates just as every other historical event: during the reign of the emperor Augustus (Luke 2:1), or during the reign of the emperor Tiberius (Luke 3:1). The same Word of God became flesh in Jesus Christ. Only a God who is Lord over time could enter into time.

Grandchild: If this is true, how should we spend our time? How should we use It?

Granddaddy: Occasionally, with time off from work or school, a young person will spend some time listening to their iPad, the radio, or television, or texting, checking their Facebook, or emailing their friends or family. Some parents say this is a waste of time. Most young people would agree that it is a time of enjoyment and relaxation. It is time well spent! Parents, of course, spend their leisure doing things they enjoy. Everyone usually finds some way to fill most of his time: working, sleeping, watching TV, texting, reading, listening to music, talking, eating, participating in or observing some sport.

Is time something simply to be used? Life itself is the creative act of God, and so is time. Time, then, would appear to be a gift that is entrusted to men and women to be used wisely and carefully. Every life is short, even at the longest life-span, and therefore needs to have direction and meaning. The ancient Greek concept of time was tragic because time was an endless cycle repeating itself again and again. What a person did to help another was futile since the stage of development soon would decay; then the cyclical rhythm would begin again. The Christian, on the other hand, views time as going somewhere and as an unrepeatable and unique event.

How often someone will say "time will heal" or "he or she will get better with time." Yet time itself is unable to bring healing or improvement. Unless there is treatment, unless there is guidance and instruction, the passing of time may make a situation worse. Time in and of itself can do nothing. It comes to us as an opportunity to be used. The response to the opportunity will determine what "time will tell."

There is no question about our responding. We respond every day. Even the decision not to answer a summons is a response. We respond just as surely by doing nothing as by choosing to do something. In fact, the decision to do nothing, given the opportunities we have, may be the costliest decision anyone can make.

Time is significant only to living creatures. It has no real importance for rocks or *dirt*. Time is important for us because it provides for us the moments in which we have opportunity to live. "This is the day which the Lord hath made; we will rejoice and be glad in it" (Psalm 118:24).

"So, teach us to number our days that we may get a heart of wisdom" (Psalm 90:12, RSV). See also Psalm 103:15; Isaiah 40:6; John 16:21. The quality of life which the Christian has found in the redemption of Christ is not something which he or she receives in the next life; it begins here in this world the moment he or she has encountered Christ. Something new has entered into our life here in this world which gives us a new sense of direction and purpose. "Therefore, if any man be in Christ, he is a new creature: old things are passed away; behold, all things are become new" (2 Corinthians 5:17). This sense of the "eternal in the present" or "life in Christ" summons us to spend our time carefully (John 4:14; 8:51-52).

Natural laws of creation

Grandchild: Sometimes the relation between God's creation and the laws of nature seem difficult to see. Miracles seem out of place and unbelievable in a climate of opinion in which history is objective facts, and facts are things which happen according to objective natural laws. How can we really understand creation as an act of God?

Granddaddy: I understand that dilemma. Think with me for a moment. Few towns in the Old West had any "sign" of law and order. At least this is the way a typical Western TV program presents the case. Outlaws ran the town without any regard for anyone or anything but themselves.

Often the world seems to be spinning like a top in a universe without any sign of law and order. Floods, earthquakes, hurricanes, tornadoes, wars, accidents, and diseases raise doubts in the minds of many people about law and order in the universe. "Where is God at times like these?" we ask.

The universe, as conceived by the ancient world view depicted in such epic poems as the *Iliad* and the *Odyssey,* was absolutely chaotic. Nothing could be trusted to remain the same, for the gods could intervene capriciously and arbitrarily in the affairs of men. Having this outlook toward the natural realm and the gods, the ancients must have lived with a sense of terror and uncertainty. Imagine the madness of the world as conceived without any sense of law, purpose, or guidance. Suppose the oak tree in our yard could change overnight into a snowman, or the moon could turn into green cheese, or the grass seed that we planted decided to come up as watermelon plants, or your car could change at will into a tricycle or a motor boat, or the car decide to go through the lake today, or the water in the nearby lake decided to turn into sawdust. Suppose we could not depend on the stability, the orderliness, of the physical world. Imagine the confusion and the hopelessness of trying to live in such a world.

Grandchild: That would be a frightening world.

Granddaddy: Yes, it would. But I don't believe that God has created such a topsy-turvy world. God has created a world with dependable laws, and continues to sustain it with divine power and grace: "God, ... upholding all things by the word of his power" (Hebrews 1:1,3). Although the world has been created as a law-abiding universe, God has allowed freedom within this order. The apostle Paul says that "the creation itself will be set free from its bondage to decay. . . We know that the whole creation has been groaning in travail together until now" (Romans 8:21-22, RSV). The Genesis creation account declares that God looked on his creation and observed that it was "good," not perfect. Both man and the universe are moving toward fulfilment (Psalm 65:6-13; Acts 17:28; Colossians1:17).

God has created us with a free will. God has not made us as a robot or a puppet. In our use of the freedom God has given us in creation, we are expected, however, to learn how *to* live in cooperation with the created or natural laws of the universe. If a person jumps off a fifty-story building, he cannot change his mind halfway down. The law of gravity will be enforced. If a child runs into the street in front of an automobile, she will get hurt or possibly will be killed. When parents teach their children not to play with matches, or to keep their hands off a hot stove, or not to play in the street, or not to play with razor blades, are they undermining the will and laws of God? Instead of being opposed to God's will, are they not attempting to teach their children to live in association with the natural laws in a dependable universe? When someone gets burned, cut, hurt, or killed, should we call this the intention or the will of God? Instead of being the will of God, these appear to be the result of a willful abuse of the divine laws of the universe. God expects us to learn how to live in the universe. God has given every person a free will and does not deny anyone the expression of it; through its expression we sometimes get hurt.

Disasters and Accidents

Grandchild: But what about disasters in nature? Does God send them?

Granddaddy: Even in natural calamities the universe is operating in a reliable way. An earthquake is the natural process for the settling of the earth's surface. Hurricanes are the natural results of certain atmospheric formations. These occurrences are according to natural laws, and sometimes people get hurt because they happen to be in the path of the natural operation of the universe. We need to distinguish between what God "causes" or "allows" because of the natural working of the universe according to law and order, and what God "intends" as God's ultimate will. If any one person could change the natural laws to suit his own whims, then there would be no order in the world for anyone. Without a universe which is dependable and basically predictable, you and I could never become a free and responsible person. We must learn to live with the freedom in God's orderly universe.

Miracles

Grandchild: A friend told me recently about the time his brother was in an accident. He said that he can still see the doctor moving slowly away from the side of his brother's bed and looking out over the city from the hospital window. After momentarily gazing over the sleeping city, he turned to the parents and spoke deliberately: "Your son is in critical condition. The car was almost demolished on impact, and Wayne was crushed severely. Only a miracle could save him now!" What did the doctor mean? Do we turn to God for divine assistance only when every other resource has failed? What about miracles? Do they really happen? Can we really believe in them in our scientific world today?

Granddaddy: Imagine what a man or a woman who lived three thousand or even a hundred years ago might think if he or she could see the world as it is today. What would he think of cars, trains, electric lights, television, telephones, elevators, air-conditioned houses, airplanes, computers, smart phones, and the thousand and one things everyone today takes for granted? He would think he was living in a world of miracles. And in a sense, he would be. Our age appears to be an age of miracles. Man, himself or woman herself is one of the greatest miracles.

Within the human body is a fuel that pumps approximately seventy times a minute. The human brain is the most complex of all computers. Our eyes, ears, voices, arms, and are skillfully constructed. The changing of the seasons, the birth of a child, the growth of a tree, the falling of rain--all of these are evidence that creation itself is in a sense a miracle.

The miracle accounts in the Bible continue to be a source of controversy for many young people. Some say: "I just can't believe them." Others remark: "I do not understand them." Before any person pushes them aside as peripheral and unimportant, especially the miracle stories of the Gospels, he would be wise to consider the high proportion of the Gospel record that is concerned with them. Nearly one third of the Gospel of Mark alone deals with the miracles of Jesus. The four Gospels tell of thirty-five miracles by Jesus. Some are given in great length, while others are referred to briefly.

The miracles of Jesus were not just tacked on to add effect but constitute an essential part of the Gospel records. When Jesus spoke in the synagogue in Nazareth, he opened his ministry with the claim: "The Spirit of the Lord is upon me, because he hath anointed me to preach the *gospel* to the poor; he hath sent me to heal the brokenhearted, to preach deliverance to the captives, and recovering of sight to the blind, to set at liberty them that are bruised" (Luke 4:18). Jesus was frequently surrounded by people who wanted him to heal them (Matthew 15:30; Mark 3:10; Luke 6:18). Matthew described the ministry of Jesus with these words: "He went about all Galilee, teaching in their synagogues and preaching the gospel of the kingdom and healing every disease and every infirmity among the people" (Matthew 4:23, RSV). His miracles constituted a vital part of his whole life and teaching.

Grandchild: What is a miracle? How can we understand them?

Granddaddy: To define a miracle is no easy task. If one believes in God, and believes that God not only created the world but continues to sustain it, the problem is not as acute. However, if a person does not believe in God, then that person certainly will not accept any definition of miracles as valid. Leslie D. Weatherhead, a noted English preacher in the last century, has suggested a helpful definition. "A miracle is a law-abiding event by which God accomplishes His redemptive purposes through the release of energies which belong to a plane of being higher than any with which we are normally familiar."

Philosophers like Spinoza and Hume, who were skeptical about miracles, usually criticized them as a violation of natural law. Miracles, however, are not events that break or change the natural laws of the universe. Jesus was not seeking to work in opposition to his Father's natural laws but was seeking to work in harmony with his Father. "The Son can do nothing of himself, but what he sees the Father do: for what things so ever he does, these also does the Son likewise" (John 5:19). "The Father that dwells in me, he does the works" (John 14:10). Miracles are not the breaking of natural laws but are lesser laws of nature giving way to higher laws, or weaker laws giving place to stronger ones. When an airplane rises three thousand feet into the sky, this does not mean that the law of gravity no longer is operative. It means simply that the plane has used a different combination of natural laws to allow it to suspend the law of gravity. C. S. Lewis calls miracles and their impact on the natural laws the revealing of the "rules behind the rules, and a unity which is deeper than uniformity."

God is not controlled by the universe; God directs it. Even within the past few years many new operations within nature have been discovered by science. Mutations and the strange operations of the atom are new scientific discoveries that continue to puzzle the scientists. Jesus Christ was on the highest spiritual plane anyone could be on in relationship to the Creator. He was able to draw out of this relationship spiritual power which was on a level that exceeded that of normal experience. This higher spiritual principle, I believe, did not violate natural laws but superseded them as a higher law.

Jesus refused to work miracles to compel men and women to believe in him as divine, or to satisfy the curiosity of the Pharisees (Mark 8:12; Matthew 12:39; Luke 11:16; John 12:44-50). His miracles were not just tricks of magic to dazzle and bewilder his followers, Jesus' miracles or "mighty works" were understood by him and others as "signs" (Matthew 11: 2-6; Luke 7:16; Acts 2:22). The characteristic word that the Gospel of John uses to describe the miracles of Jesus is "sign. (John 4:54; 7:31; 9:16). The other Gospel writers also regard the miracles as having a deeper meaning than just a physical healing or action. To those who had eyes to see, Jesus' miracles were "signs" (Mark 8:18; Luke 10:23). They could not compel belief, but to the believer they were "signs" of the mystery of the kingdom of God (Mark 4:11). The miracles of Jesus were "signs" of the power and compassion within his heart for man, "signs" of God's concern for man as he *has* revealed his love through Jesus Christ (Matthew 11:20-23; Luke 7:13). Jesus' miracles were performed, not that men and women would be amazed by the marvelous acts, but to point them beyond the literal acts themselves to the God who was revealing himself in and through his Son.

Grandchild: Go a little further and explain what you mean by miracles as a sign and especially how this relates to Jesus?

Granddaddy: Good question, I'll try and clarify what I mean. Life is full of signs: "Keep Off the Grass," "Walk," "Go," "Wait," "Stop," "Children at Play," "School Zone," and a thousand others. Some signs warn or caution; others guide or inform. All of them seek to convey some truth in a clear, unambiguous way. The important thing is not the sign itself; it points beyond itself to guide or inform. The miracles recorded in the Gospels are also "signs" that point beyond the actual occurrences to the world's central event. The central sign of the ages is seen in Jesus Christ. He was the world's greatest miracle because he was the grand "sign" that revealed the "very face of the Most high."

The incarnation of God in Jesus Christ is the event upon which the Christian faith is founded. Without question the incarnation is the central doctrine of the Christian church. In Christ, the "impossible possibility" has occurred. "God was in Christ, reconciling the world unto himself" (2 Corinthians 5:19). In Jesus Christ, God has spoken of himself in the greatest revelation or "central sign." The greatness of the Christian religion is not mere talk, words, or ideas but that "the Word became flesh." Here is the gospel in a nutshell. This concept contains the essence of the world's greatest miracle: The eternal God focused God's self in Jesus Christ. In the incarnation, C. S. Lewis claims, is a new key principle: "the power of the Higher, just in so far as it is truly Higher, to come down, the power of the Greater to include the less."

The biblical writers were bold enough to assert that Christ is the fulfilment, completion, and transformer of all creation. The incarnation gives meaning and purpose to all of creation. In his epistle to the Colossians Paul made this concept clear: "He is the image of the invisible God, the first-born of all creation; for in him all things were created, in heaven and on earth, visible and invisible, . . . all things were created through him and for him. He is before all things, and in him all things hold together .... For in him all the fulness of God was pleased to dwell, and through him to reconcile to himself all things, whether on earth or in heaven, making peace by the blood of his cross" (Colossians 1:15-20, RSV).

The Incarnation

Grandchild: Can we ever fully clarify the incarnation?

Granddaddy: The incarnation of Christ cannot really be explained. It will forever remain the great mystery of the Christian faith. If God has made God's presence known in a unique personal way through Jesus Christ, the deeds, teachings, and actions of his life are what one would expect from such a nature. For one who lived in perfect spiritual harmony with the Creator of the universe, the miracles from his hands are evidence of the higher spiritual communion which he shared with his Father. The life, teaching, and death of Jesus Christ are clear signs that point us to the eternal God of the universe. Jesus Christ is himself the "central sign" who reveals to men and women what the eternal God is like. " 'He who believes in me, believes not in me but in him who sent me. And he who sees me sees him who sent me'" (John 12:44-45, RSV).

Holiness of God

Grandchild: In the prayer that Jesus taught his disciples is the petition, "Hallowed be thy name" (Matthew 6:9). Few today seem very aware of the holy nature of God. Some have described God, which you told us earlier, as a "living doll," the "man upstairs," the *"big* daddy," the "bosom buddy," or "Mr. Big." I have heard it said that the fundamental act of all religion is the worship of the Holy God. If this is true, how do we approach God in a respectful and reverent way? In the Old Testament, we read that when Moses, the shepherd, approached a burning bush, he was told to take off his shoes, because he was standing on holy ground (Exodus 3: 5). Before God would speak to Moses, there had to be an attitude of reverence. How can we really understand the meaning of the holiness of God?

Granddaddy: In the Old Testament, we read about Isaiah and his striking vision of wonder and beauty. "I saw also the Lord sitting upon a throne, high and lifted up, and his train filled the temple. Above it stood the seraphims: each one had six wings, with twain he covered his face, and with twain he covered his feet, and with twain he did fly. And one cried unto another, and said, Holy, holy, holy, is the Lord of hosts: the whole earth is full of his glory" (Isaiah 6:1-3). Isaiah was overcome by God's holiness and his glory. The designation of God as the "Holy One of Israel" probably came out of Isaiah's awesome encounter with God (Isaiah 12:6; 17:7; 29:19). Many of the great hymns of worship have been patterned after the sublime worship experience of Isaiah. Believers everywhere lift their voices and sing, "Holy, Holy, Holy, is the Lord of hosts: the whole earth is full of his glory." In God's holiness lies God's divine mystery (Read Isaiah 45:15).

The basic meaning of the term translated as holiness in the Old Testament is the idea of "separation." Holiness is that quality in God which distinguishes God from every other form of existence. The holiness of God is the distinguishing factor which sets God apart from humanity, the world, and all the rest of creation (Isaiah 40:25; 57:15; Hosea 11:9; Revelation 4:8-11). In the biblical revelation, God is not described as "the Holy God" in an abstract sense, but God is always depicted as "the Holy One" who seeks to meet us personally (Isaiah 43:3; 45:11). The holiness of God is not just one of God's divine attributes, but is the essence of God's inward nature, the source and ground of God's total being. God's holiness is what constitutes God's very innermost nature as divine.

Not only is God "the Holy One," God alone is holy. Holiness is God's unique quality which belongs to God because of God's nature. Confronted by the eternal author and creator of all of life, men and women can simply declare, "Thou only art holy" (Revelation 15:4). Holiness can be attributed to other things only as they derive their holiness from God. Since the basic meaning of the word for "holy" means different or separate; places, objects, and persons are holy only in the sense that they are "holy unto the Lord." A temple is holy in the sense that it is different from other buildings because of its purpose. The Lord's Day or the sabbath is holy because it is different from the other days in the week. In the Old Testament, a priest was considered holy because he was separate from other men and dedicated unto God. When Jesus taught his disciples to pray "Hallowed be thy name," he was declaring that God's name is to be treated differently from every other name (Matthew 6:9). God's nature demands an absolute unique position. Whenever we attribute holiness to an object independent of God, we are committing idolatry, I believe.

Grandchild: I do believe that God alone is holy. What are some of the characteristics of the Holiness of God?

Granddaddy: Many terms are used in the Bible in association with holiness. The imagery of fire is one of the earliest and the one most frequently attributed to "the Holy One." Light, flame, burn, glow, and other terms related to fire are used to describe the holiness of God (Exodus 3:23; Deuteronomy 5:22-27; Psalm 18:8-14; Matthew 3:11; Acts 2:1-4). In all the biblical images of "the Holy One," the *mystery* of God's nature is apparent. No one can fully know God's ways or God's thoughts. God is *incomprehensible* to man and woman (1 Corinthians 2:11; Job 11:3-12; Psalm 139:6). God is also *incomparable*. No figure, image, description, or word is adequate to completely describe God (Isaiah 40:25).

In God's holiness, God is *wholly other.* Our sinfulness separates us from God. Even at our very best, we must realize that a great chasm separates us from God. Since God's nature is so radically different from ours, the initiative in revelation and redemption comes from God, not us. God bridged the chasm caused by our sin. No one approaches "the Holy One" (Exodus 3:5; 33:20; Hosea 11:9; Psalm 9:20). The ethical transcendence of God was seen by Isaiah when he was made aware that God's way transcends our human way (Isaiah 55:8-9). Although God is transcendent, the qualities of mercy and redemption are found in his holiness (Isaiah 52:10; Psalm 98:2; Hebrews 8:11). In the Old Testament "the Holy One" of Israel is the redeeming God that delivered Israel from Egypt (Exodus 20:2). In the New Testament, the Holy Spirit spreads God's love in the hearts of men and women (Romans 5:5).

As "the Holy One," God is also exalted and sublime, fearsome and awesome, wonderful, and great, unique, and mighty, hidden and revealing (Psalms 89:7; 95:3; Isaiah 33:5; Job 42:3; Exodus 33:20). In the concept of God's holiness, there is apparent an element of separation and inclusion. We are radically different from God, and when we attempt to come into God's presence, we are immediately aware of our sinfulness and God's holiness. We are unable to stand before God without crying with Isaiah: "Woe is me! For I am undone; ... for mine eyes have seen the King, the Lord of hosts" (Isaiah 6:5). Sin stands in opposition to the character of God's holiness and, therefore, we must seek to defeat this power that stands opposed to God's holy desire and purpose. But as soon as we are aware of the separation caused by our sin, we are made conscious of God's welcome. The holy, blazing light which reveals the gulf that separates us from God, also reveals the bridge that unites us and God. God's redeeming love is revealed in the midst of his holiness. The prophet Hosea was among the first to declare this truth. In Jesus Christ, holiness and love are unveiled and we can see the reality of God's nature in him (Hosea 6:1-6; Isaiah 54:5; John 17:11).

Being a Saint

Grandchild: Sometimes people speak about someone being a saint. Does that mean they have become somehow holy?

Granddaddy: Suppose I asked you: "Are you a saint?" The answer to that question is usually the same. Almost no one would classify himself or herself as a saint. Many, on the other hand, would say that they try to do their best, and seek to be honest. They go to church, pray daily, and attempt to live a Christian life. But not for a moment would they claim to be a saint. Yet, the New Testament proclaims that all Christians are saints.

The word "Christian" appears only three times in the New Testament, but the word "saint" is used in reference to the Christians in the early churches. The apostle Paul, in writing to the church at Rome states: "To all that be in Rome, beloved of God, called to be saints" (Romans 1:7). Paul addressed his letters to the Corinthians, Colossians, Ephesians, and others, to all the "saints" in the churches. These letters were not sent to a select group of particular pious Christians among the churches, but they were meant for everyone in the church who was a Christian. In fifteen of the twenty-seven New Testament writings, Christians are called saints. In the New Testament, all Christians are spoken of as saints, holy men and women. Christians are saints because they are "in Christ," who is the "Holy One of God." The Christian is committed to Christ and is called to a life of consecration. In the New Testament the words for "holy" and "saint" are the same. In some passages, it is translated from the Greek one way and differently in another place. The Christian has been called to a new life. He or she has been called to be "holy" or to be a "saint."

The reference to Christians as saints does not mean that all Christians are without sin. The letters written by Paul were addressed to "saints" but they certainly had their blemishes, weaknesses, sins, and perversions. A saint is not a perfect person who is free of all sin. A saint is one who is "set apart" and committed to the Christ-like way. Paul, who was certainly one of the greatest Christians of the early church, was aware of his own sins. But he stated that "I count not myself to have apprehended: but ... I press toward the mark for the prize of the high calling of God in Christ Jesus" (Philippians 3:13-14). As a *saint,* Paul had not reached perfection, but he was striving every day to grow more like his Master. He anticipated that the Christians in the Philippian church and all the other churches would be moving toward the same goal.

Grandchild: Does that mean, if I am a Christian, I am an oddball or so different that I really can't fit in with ordinary people?

Granddaddy: That is an interesting question. Does it seem to you that almost everybody is trying to keep up with the "Joneses," whoever they are and wherever they are? Young people also follow their own "Joneses." The tendency today is to be like everybody else. Do not be different. No one wants to be considered a "square," a "prude," a "stick in the mud," a "grind," or a "wet blanket." So, most young people listen to the same music, read the same books, dress alike, look alike, sound alike, and act alike. There is a real fear of being different. To a degree, it is fine to follow normal patterns of likes and dislikes, but for the Christian there needs to be a standard that is higher than "everybody is doing it."

Jesus Christ, the Holy One of God, has called the Christian into a new way of life (1 Peter 1:15-16). The Christian saints are those who are set apart, who are called to be different. Often the Christian is not distinguishable from the rest of society. He or she ceases to be the one who is changing the world, but has been changed by it (Romans 12:2).

The saints are the light of the world, the salt of the earth, the leaven that enriches the dough. The Christians are to be the transforming factor that changes the world to the image of God. Christian holiness is a quality of life that comes from the indwelling Christ. The new birth marks the beginning of the Christian's life and is an accomplished fact. But it is the *beginning* of one's life and not the *end* of it. Christian holiness or sanctification is never something that is complete. It is a goal toward which the Christian is constantly moving. When a person encounters Christ, his or her life should have changed. The new life cannot be compartmentalized. A young person cannot say, "God, you may have this part of my life but not another." Spiritual growth extends into all the areas of life. A saint cannot hang up his religion with his Sunday clothes. Christianity is an invasion of one's whole life.

Grandchild: This seems like an almost impossible goal. Does reaching for it remove all joy and pleasure in life and leave us as the grim-faced persons in society?

Granddaddy: Christ has revealed the holy love of God, and the demand upon the Christian is to "keep up" with this holiness of God. "Be ye holy; for I am holy" (1 Peter 1:16). Christ has set before the Christian a goal that is always before us causing us to reach up to the standard of God's holiness. "Be ye therefore perfect, even as your Father which is in heaven is perfect" (Matthew 5:48). We will never fully reach the goal but continuing to strive for it.

To follow the pattern of holiness that Jesus has set for us does not mean, I believe, that all joy and happiness have gone from life. The late English writer, C. S. Lewis, in recounting the story of his conversion experience, entitled his autobiography, *Surprised by Joy.* The title is descriptive of the great joy that one finds in the Christian life. The New Testament rings with the joy that was felt in the coming of Christ. The angels declared the "good tidings of great joy" which would be for "all people" (Luke 2:10). Jesus came into the world to make known the "abundant life," and that his joy might be established in the hearts of men and women (John 15:11). As young people follow Christ, the Holy One of God, the joy and gladness that comes from being a person made whole by God's grace will become clearer. It is an inner joy that will affect everything one says, thinks, desires, and does.

To summarize our discussion here, we might reflect this way. As we experience the holiness of God, we are met by a call to excellence. This demand places upon the Christian an imperative to dedication, self-discipline, concentration, high morality, integrity, honesty, and commitment of life to the Christ-like way. Saints are those who are trying to keep up with their Master and not with the next-door neighbors or some celebrities. The holiness of God, which the character of Christ has revealed, stands as the goal and pattern toward which each Christian's life is directed. The way to holiness begins in a surrender of life to the One who is holy, God. But the goal of holiness also lies constantly before the Christian. It will require a continuous commitment and consecration. All Christians are saints, but saints who are daily being remade in the image of God.

The faithfulness of God

Grandchild: We are told that we need to have faith if we are to be true believers. Is faith really possible?

Granddaddy: Did you ever consider how much of our daily living is dependent on faith? We put our trust in the alarm clock or a smart phone to awaken us each morning. We put our lives in the hands of others as we eat the food contained in packages, cans, and frozen containers. When we ride on a bus, train, or plane, we commit our lives to the safety of the driver, the engineer, or the pilot. We trust our doctors, dentists, and druggists with our lives and health almost daily. In case of trouble we depend on our policemen and lawyers to protect us. We put our money in the bank, in faith that it will be there when we want it. The letter you wrote last night and dropped in the mail slot has been entrusted to the post office for safe delivery. We entrust our minds to our teachers and professors, confident that they will give us sound instruction. Every marriage is built on trust and fidelity, and children trust parents to meet their needs. You sat down in that chair in confidence that it would support you. We put our trust daily, hourly, and even every minute in people, gadgets, machines, maps, books, and countless other things.

Our lives are lived each day in mutual trust and confidence. Faith is the "bridge" we travel on when we cross over the chasm of uncertainty doubt, and confusion. I believe that we can trust because of our awareness of a deeper faithfulness that is the ground or foundation of all confidence. The faithfulness of God is the basis of the stability of the universe outside of us, within us, and between men and women.

Grandchild: Where does this sense of faithfulness come from?

Granddaddy: Even a casual reading through the Bible will disclose that the faithfulness of God is one of the most conspicuous themes. In a world of constant change and broken promises, God's character denotes unchangeableness and constancy. God is faithful in God's inner nature and is faithful in keeping God's promises, and is, therefore, worthy of trust. God finishes what God begins, and does not change in God's intention. To speak of God's faithfulness is simply a means to depict God's moral nature; God is always consistent with God's own ethical being. The unchangeableness of God is one way of trying to describe the harmonious character of God within God's self and in relation with us. God alone "endures to all generations" (Psalm 100:5).

God's faithfulness is grounded in God's own nature. God cannot be untrue to God's self (2 Timothy 2:13). God's faithfulness or unchangeable nature indicates that external factors cannot alter God's inner essence. God is the same because God is self-existent and eternal. "I am the Lord, I change not" (Malachi 3:6). In Exodus 3:14, where the name of God is revealed as "I AM THAT I AM," the self-existence, eternal nature, and unchangeable faithfulness of God are involved in the disclosing of God's name. Just as God had been faithful in God's promises to Abraham, Isaac, and Jacob, God would continue in God's fidelity to Moses and his people. God's faithfulness caused the psalmist to sing praises to God (Psalms 36:5; 92:2). God's faithfulness is the basis for human trust in God for salvation, security, answered prayers, and for strength in temptation (Psalms 91:4; 143:1; 1 Corinthians 10:13; 2 Thessalonians 3:3). The faithfulness of men and women often stands in sharp contrast to God's fidelity. Our infidelity, nevertheless, cannot make void God's gracious promises and faithfulness. God's promises do not depend ultimately on us; and though every person be false and untrue, God remains constant. "Let God be true, but every man a liar" (Romans 3: 4). In James 1:17 God is depicted as "the Father of lights, with whom is no variableness, neither shadow of turning." God's word stands forever.

We are also aware of the faithfulness of God in the nature of our universe. God has created our universe so that it is a law-abiding realm. Think of the chaotic state the world would be in if there were no lawful forces in the universe upon which we could depend. Suppose you could not be sure that the chair on which you are seated would remain on the floor; or whether your book would stay on the desk; or whether the chandeliers would remain hanging about you. As Dr. J. S. Whale exclaims: "If water might suddenly freeze in midsummer; if the specific gravity of lead might at any time become that of thistledown; if pigs might fly or the White House turn into Green cheese-man's life would be a nightmare. " Chaos would exist without a law-abiding universe. But God, who is constant in God's self, is the ground of all faithfulness. The faithfulness of the natural realm itself, is rooted in the One who is "the same yesterday, and today, and forever" (Hebrews 13:8).

Grandchild: Do we find this concept of God's faithfulness in the Old Testament?

Granddaddy: In the Old Testament, the idea of the covenant is one of the most central features in the relation of the nation Israel and God. The covenant was a compact or a pledge made between God and Israel. It was in no way a legal contract, but a pledge of faithfulness by Israel to God who had first chosen and redeemed her. Out of God's grace, God had delivered Israel from her bondage in Egypt and had pledged God's faithfulness to God's Chosen People. The terms of the covenant were fixed by God and God's pledge of loyalty had been demonstrated in the

Exodus. God's faithfulness and steadfast love could be relied upon; God would be true to God's contract (Deuteronomy 7:6-9).

Throughout the history of Israel, the covenant is repeatedly renewed in various places and circumstances: (1) at Ebal by Joshua (Joshua 8:30), (2) by Josiah (2 Kings 23:3), and (3) by Ezra and Nehemiah (Ezra 10:3; Nehemiah 8:1-2). It is a mistaken idea, however, to assume that God's covenant with Israel bound God to the nation to such a degree that the people could not break the pledge. The fact is that the covenant called for the continued loyalty and obedience of the nation, and without this renewal of commitment Israel's contract would be broken and repudiated. God would not be unfaithful to the nation, but the covenant was based on the loyalty of the nation to God and God's laws (Exodus 19:5).

The privilege of being God's people carried with it the responsibility of remaining faithful to God. Privilege involves obligation. Even when the nation was unfaithful, God attempted to restore their faithfulness. The prophets declared the unfailing love of God toward God's people and tried to call them back to loyalty and service (Jeremiah 25:4; Hosea 11:8). The disloyalty to the covenant is given as the reason the nation had to go into exile. And because the old covenant had been broken by the sins of the people, God made a new covenant after the exile which would be written in the hearts of men and women. In the new covenant, not just the nation, but individual persons would be bound to God by love and grace (Jeremiah 31:31-33; Hosea 3).

Grandchild: Aren't we as Christians expected to be faithful to Christ?

Granddaddy: That's an important question. First, a story. During the off-season, a lumberjack was converted to Christ. He became worried about what his old cronies might say when they found out that he had "got religion," so he decided to ask his pastor for advice. His pastor told him to be a Christian in everything he did. He left for camp and spent the season working. At the end of the season he returned home and when he was asked how he got along, he beamed: "Just fine! Nobody ever found out that I was a Christian."

The lack of genuine Christian commitment on the part of many church members is one of the most serious problems confronting the church today. Just as men and women were bound by a cord of faithfulness to God in the Old Testament understanding of the covenant, we are now bound by a commitment of faith to Jesus Christ in the new covenant. The old covenant is fulfilled in the new covenant, and God's faithfulness has been revealed through God's Son. The Christian life is a commitment to be a faithful disciple of Jesus Christ (2 Corinthians 3:1-6; Hebrews 9:15). The Christian today needs to affirm: "For I am proud of the gospel; it is God's saving power for everyone who has faith." (Romans 1:16, Moffatt)

God has imparted to the Christian a great trust. God has given to us the gospel to share with the world, a gospel of good news of redeeming grace for all persons. In one of the parables of Jesus, a man was praised for his faithfulness. "Well done, you good and faithful servant: you have been faithful over a few things, I will make you ruler over many things: enter into the joy of thy Lord" (Matthew 25:21). Fidelity *is* essential on the part of the believer if the good news is to be shared. Someone has said that Christianity is always just one generation away from extinction. It is the responsibility of this present generation to bear witness to Christ. Keith Miller, a writer, of some years ago, compares the person who does not share the gospel to a hospital patient who has been cured of a dread disease, but who only walks among the other sick patients and refuses to share *his* healing knowledge with them. There is no place for neutrality as a Christian witness; not to share with another the grace one has received in Christ is equivalent to extinguishing it (Matthew 28:19-20; Acts 1:8).

Grandchild: My friend, Sam, says that he does not need to speak about Christ in any verbal way; he will simply let his life bear witness. Mary, a school mate, is convinced that no one's life is effective without a spoken word. What do you think about their argument?

Granddaddy: I think we are called to be faithful to the end. Some people can begin a new undertaking, but often they lack the staying power to finish the task. Most marriages begin in a burst of enthusiastic love, but it requires a growing sense of devotion to make a lasting home. A career can begin in an ardent desire to reach the top, but often it will collapse when the rungs on the business ladder get further apart. A student will undertake a new language with the hope of being able to converse in a foreign tongue, but when the necessary tedious hours of study begin to be missed, the new language is soon impossible to learn. Many a "bonus rookie" is given large sums of money to play for a team, and his possibilities make headlines on the sports page. Yet, many "rookies" are unable to meet the expectations when they are set in the midst of big league competition.

It is one thing to begin the Christian pilgrimage, and another to complete it. The parable of the sower and the soils describes the rocky soil where the seed comes up quickly and is soon gone because there is no depth of soil where real growth would be possible (Matthew 13:3-9). These people mean well. They say, "Lord, I will follow thee," but let me say farewell to the folks at home; let me finish school; let me grow up; let me get married, then I will be a Christian. These people are not willing to get off the fence and stand up and be counted for Christ. Sometimes a person will be enthusiastic about Christ; he or she will be inspired for a few moments, but the ardor soon cools and he or she falls away. The call to Christian discipleship is a call to faithfulness. "He that shall endure unto the end, the same shall be saved" (Matthew 24: 13).

In the book of Revelation, the church at Smyrna is exhorted: "Be faithful unto death, and I will give you a crown of life" (Revelation 2:10). The way of Christ is often lined with "dropout" Christians, those who begin but soon fade away. Some writers project that from one half to two thirds of those who begin to walk with Christ drop by the wayside. If one has committed his or her life to Christ, it must be a growing relationship. This does not mean that we always practice those things we fervently believe, and no one else likely does either all the time, but we must try continuously to follow the Christ-like way the best we can. With every follower of Christ, Christian growth is a necessity. Growth cannot come from a superficial or trivial relationship with Christ and his church, but is based on faithful allegiance to Christ. (Read 2 Timothy 2: 12-13).

Let me summarize our conversation this way. God's faithfulness is grounded in God's very nature. God cannot be false to God's self, and God will not be unfaithful to us. In the Old Testament the covenant made between God and Israel was dependent upon the loyalty and faithfulness of the nation. When the nation turned her back on God, God still tried to bring her back to God's love. God continues to seek out men and women even when they turn away from God's love. God's new covenant is revealed through Jesus Christ, but the call to discipleship from the Master still demands fidelity. The Christian life begins in a commitment of faith, and the believer matures as he or she continues in a faithful walk day-by-day with the eternal Lord.

Grandchild: What is love?

Granddaddy: That's a difficult question to answer in a few words. Love is one of the most powerful words in any language, and it can be used in many ways. It is used to describe the love between a man and a woman, or parents for their children, or children for their parents. A girl loves her doll and a boy loves his dog. There is also love of ice cream, hot dogs, and cokes. People often speak about the love of country, love of power, and love of wealth. There can be love without sex and sex without love. Young people talk about first love, many loves, too many loves, last love, and saddest of all, no love. People also speak about the love of God, God's love for us, the love of self, and love of others. Though the word for love may be used sometimes to express our affection for the most trivial things, love is still the greatest thing in the world. Love, when properly understood, is the only authentic word that can describe our self-understanding, our relationship with God, and our attitude toward others. Love forms a triangle in which God, self, and neighbor are bound together.

Grandchild: Through hymns, preaching, and writings much is said about the love of God. What is God's love? How is the love of God expressed in the Scriptures and in human life? How does experiencing the love of God help in discovering positive feeling about self, others, and God?

Granddaddy: If each of us is to locate the center of his or her own life, he or she must understand what the nature of the force is like at the center of the universe. The biblical answer to this dilemma states that the axis at the center around which the world and humanity revolves is the love of God. The biblical concept of God's love cannot be defined in an exhaustive way. Love itself is an evasive concept and when this concept is linked with the being of God, it becomes even more difficult to describe. Any statement about the characteristics of God's love cannot be complete, but it can serve to point out certain known qualities.

In the Old Testament, the idea of divine love is expressed in various ways. The highest Hebrew word for divine love is usually translated "loving-kindness" or "steadfast love." Often the word "faithfulness" is used with "loving-kindness" to denote that God is loyal and good, like a close friend. The idea of divine love was expressed in the covenant relation between God and Israel. The covenant love represented the faithful love of God toward the Chosen People. The pledge or compact that God made with Israel to love them was conditioned upon their obedience. Hosea was probably the first to present the highest concept of God in the Old Testament. He pictured Israel as the bride of God whose love was both merciful and firm.

The First Epistle of John presents one of the highest utterances in the Bible concerning God. "God is love" (1 John 4:8,16). Love originates from God and is centered in God's nature. All genuine love finds its source in God and is a reflection of God's inner love. Since God is spirit, we cannot see God with our visible eyes, but the effect of God's love can be visible in the hearts and lives of people everywhere. God's love is not a temporary expression of the divine nature, but is an eternal quality of God's being. God is eternal, and since God is love, God's love is also eternal. God is no absentee landlord who has been twiddling his thumbs throughout eternity. God has always been loving. In Jesus Christ, we have seen God's eternal love expressed within time. The cross does not represent an isolated moment of love, but is a translation into history of an eternal fact. The grace and love of God revealed in Jesus of Nazareth is the revelation of the eternal nature of the love and grace of God who has always been seeking to make God's presence known and acknowledged by men and women.

Everything God does is consistent with God's nature as love. Love was the motive for the act of creation. Through divine creative activity, God was able to express God's desire for fellowship. God's creative love always desires the highest good for creation. Love is the stimulus for God's redemption. God is not content that we simply suffer the consequences of our sins, but God is a seeking and forgiving God. God's compassion, grace, and mercy are expressions of divine love for us. In the life and death of Jesus Christ, God has revealed the nature of divine love. God's patience, mercy, graciousness, forgiveness, and sacrificial love have been manifested in Christ. God's love is not limited to any one nation, race, or group, but is extended to include all those who will share in God's fellowship. Frederick Faber has expressed it well in his hymn: "There's a wideness in God's mercy, Like the wideness of the sea."

Grandchild: What does Jesus teach us about love?

Granddaddy: God's love is always striving to reach men and women, but it must find a lodging place within us. When Jesus was asked, what was the first and greatest of the commandments, he declared, "Hear, O Israel; The Lord our God is one Lord: and you shall love the Lord the God with all your heart, and with all your soul, and with all your mind, and with all your strength: this is the first commandment. And the second is like, namely this, you shall love your neighbor as yourself. There is no other commandment greater than these" (Mark 12:29-31). How like Jesus to focus our attention on the essentials of religion! In these two commandments Jesus reduced the whole rabbinic system of 613 commands, 248 positive ones and 365 prohibitions, into two. Jesus strips away the complexity of the law and makes bare the simplicity at the center. What Jesus gives us is "religion in a nutshell."

He focuses our attention on "first things first." These two commandments clearly indicate what is supposed to have precedence in our lives.

The first commandment that Jesus stated was a part of the *Shema,* which was and still is the center of the Hebrew creed. This commandment is first because man's love for God conditions his love for himself, his family, and all others. It is a call to love God with one's total being and personality. Our emotions, intellect, thoughts, and energy are to be totally committed to God. Jesus has indicated that everyone must direct her loyalty; it cannot be divided. "No person can serve two masters" (Matthew 6:24). "But seek first the kingdom of God" (v. 33).

Grandchild: But can the love of God be commanded?

Granddaddy: The starry skies above, the order in creation, the beauty in acts of kindness and compassion, the mysterious voice within, all seem to indicate a call to obedience. But a person is able to obey the call to love God, because he or she is aware of God's prior love for us. (1 John 4:19) The command to love God means a deliberate directing of one's will to respond to divine love. As C. H. Dodd, a New Testament scholar, has observed: "Our very capacity to love, whether the object of our love be God or our neighbor, is given to us in the fact of our being loved by God." Love begins in God and extends outward to us, and then we reply by reaching up in a responsive love to God.

Grandchild: I sometimes wonder if it is possible to love myself?

Granddaddy: The Greek philosopher, Socrates, taught as the first law of learning, "to know yourself." But how do we know ourselves? Who is this creature called man/woman? How often we say or hear others say: "I don't feel myself today"; "I must have been out of my mind"; "I'm ashamed of myself"; "I forgot myself"; "I hate myself for doing that"; "I must pull myself together." The struggle today is for each of us to know himself or herself. The new emphasis is on depth-psychology. The old cry was "Westward-ho" but now it is "in-ward-ho." The new quest is to know what makes a person tick; what causes her to be the way she is. Often, we are a civil war, within. Pride, lust, greed, fear, and other traits demand first place in our lives and there seems to be nowhere to turn. As one novelist has expressed it, "Man against himself." Man/woman has lost his/her polestar.

Shakespeare's *Hamlet* reminds us: "This above all: to thine own self be true, and it must follow, as the night the day, thou canst not then be false to any man." But which self is the true one? Luke speaks of the change in the prodigal son "when he came to himself" (Luke 15:17). Jesus has told us to love our neighbors as ourselves. But what is proper self-love? Freud called love of self "narcissism." This is the type of self-love that causes one to admire himself. He is the guy who is "stuck on himself." But this is not the self-love of which Jesus is speaking. To love oneself in the biblical sense is to fulfil the potential for which God has created us. Proper self-love demands a healthy respect for one's own personhood. Self-respect rises out of the awareness that we have been created in "the image of God." The worth God holds for each person has been indicated by the life, suffering, and death of Christ.

Grandchild: But isn't selfishness wrong?

Granddaddy: Selfishness is self-love misdirected. Proper self-love constantly denies itself so the higher self might grow. Jesus has called us to a higher law than the maxim: "Self-preservation is the first law of nature." In a paradoxical statement, Jesus declared: "Whosoever will save his life shall lose it: but whosoever will lose his life for my sake, the same shall save it" (Luke 9:24). The emphasis is not how much a person can *get* out of life but on how much he or she can *give*. Life is not to be hoarded for self but is to be spent in service for Christ.

Proper self-love is found, I believe, in directing the will to reach the goal which God has for us. Jesus has called his followers to be "perfect even as your Father which is in heaven is perfect" (Matthew 5:48). The Greek word for "perfect" means an end, a purpose, an aim, or a goal. The Greek idea of perfection is functional. A thing is perfect if it attains the purpose for which it was made. We were created to live in fellowship with God. To love self properly is to be aware of this high goal God has for each life. The characteristics of the higher self are given in 1 Corinthians 13. Exemplified fully only in Jesus Christ, these characteristics are part of the goal toward which the Christian is moving in his or her quest for genuine selfhood. Since God has made us, loved us, and redeemed us, we need to maintain a high regard for our own personhood. By being aware of what we can be and should be in God's love, we are able to achieve genuine personhood through the surrender of self to God.

Grandchild: Can we think about love merely for ourselves and not be concerned about the needs of others?

Granddaddy: Matthew's presentation of the First Commandment reads: "You shall love the Lord your God with all your heart, and with. all your soul, and with all your mind. This is the first and great commandment. And the second is like unto it. You shall love your neighbor as yourself" (Matthew 22:37-39). Jesus put these two commandments (Leviticus 19:18; Deuteronomy 6:5) together and made them one. Love toward God and others are inseparable. The love that we experience in God's salvation is indeed an intensely personal matter, but it can never be merely a private matter and no more. No one is ever an isolated ego. Love for God must always issue outward in love toward others. Not being an isolated ego, we express our love of God only in relation to others. Religion and morality can never be separated. A person's life can reflect love toward God by extending unselfish love toward one's fellowman and woman.

In the Johannine epistle, the following statement is descriptive of a person's love toward God: "If a man says, I love God, and hates his brother, he is a liar: for he that loves not his brother whom he has seen, how can he love God whom he has not seen? And this commandment have we from him, that he who loves God love his brother also" (1 John 4:20-21). We cannot love God in an abstract way, but we love God in and through our fellowmen and women. Who are our neighbors and our brothers? Since all persons have been created in the image of God, God's love reaches out to embrace all persons. Jesus even goes beyond the Old Testament law of "an eye for an eye," and commands that we love our enemies and pray for those who persecute us. (Read Matthew 5:44). The fact that Jesus could ask for the forgiveness of those who put him on the cross is convincing testimony to his revelation of what divine love is like (Luke 23:34). It means little to say that one loves God if she does not show it in her attitude toward others. The Christian, like his Master, has come to minister and not to be ministered unto. Worship is an end in itself; but it does not end in itself. Worship and service are inseparable. In his description of the last judgment, Jesus indicates clearly that the redeemed will be those who have demonstrated their love for God by ministering to the hungry, the strangers, the sick, the poor, and others in need (Matthew 25:31-46). The command to love God and neighbor stands or falls together.

It is often said that "love is what makes the world go round." This can be true only to the extent that love is at the center of one's life. To continue moving in a circle without a goal or purpose is to live a meaningless existence. When life finds its center in God's love, this love conditions all the other areas of life. The length, the width. the height, and the depth of God's love will always surpass human knowledge. But out of this love will come our understanding of one's self and our attitude and actions toward others. George Matheson's hymn expresses it well. "O Love that wilt not let me go, I rest my weary soul in thee; I give thee back the life I owe. That in thine ocean depths its flow May richer, fuller be."

Grandchild: Can a name have any significance in religion?

Granddaddy: Romeo once asked: "What's in a name?" Parents raise that question when a new baby arrives, "What shall we call him or her?" Today, a name is little more than an identification tag. It is a way one person is distinguished from another. In the ancient Hebrew thinking, a person's name indicated his or her personality and nature. To know God's name meant to know something of God's reality. When Moses asked God the question: "When I come to the children of Israel, and shall say unto them, The God of your fathers has sent me unto you; and they shall say *to* me, what is his name? what shall I say unto them?" The answer was, "I AM THAT I AM: ... has sent me unto you" (Exodus 3:13-14). God alone is; all others have been and shall be. The name of God reveals God's eternal nature and the life and power that is available to those who serve God.

In the announcement of the birth of Christ, the Gospel of Matthew declares that his name shall be called "Jesus: for he shall save his people from their sins." He will be named "Emmanuel, which being interpreted is, God with us" (Matthew 1:21,23). The apostle Paul states that "God was in Christ; reconciling the world unto himself" (2 Corinthians 5:19). The incarnation of God in Jesus Christ is the fundamental tenet of the Christian faith. In Jesus Christ, the very "face of the Most High" has been revealed. The essence of God's nature has been disclosed in the "Word that became flesh." The late John Baillie is correct when he wrote concerning 2 Corinthians 5:19: "This is the declaration on which the Christian religion is founded. We call it the doctrine of the Incarnation, and there is no question that it is the central doctrine of the Christian faith."

What is in a name? In the name and person of Jesus Christ, God has been revealed. God has been revealed as a loving Father, who is near and available, who cares for the welfare of God's children, and who desires to have intimate fellowship with them. Jesus called God "Father," and through the Son the Father's nature has been revealed.

God as Father

Grandchild: Can we still use the term "Father" for God today?

Granddaddy: I believe that what Jesus told us about God might well be summed up in the name "Father." Father was the name Jesus used to address God. It was a name which was expressive of his close and intimate relationship to God. Although Jesus breathed into the term a breath of new meaning and content, he was not the first to call God "Father." In Greek mythology, for example, Zeus is depicted as the father of the gods, and in Roman mythology, Father Jupiter is ranked the highest. Here, divine father is merely the name for the god of the highest rank in a chain of other gods. This idea of divine fatherhood represents God as the physical giver of life. He is the Father who has produced the human race in a physical sense.

In the Old Testament, the fatherhood of God is often presented. Usually it refers to the nation Israel as the elected child of God the Father. God is Father to Israel in the sense that God has adopted them. But God's act. of adoption demands an obedient response, and only those who are obedient to God are truly God's children (Exodus 4:22; Psalm 103:13). "A son honors his father, and a servant his master: if then I be a father, where is mine honor?" (Malachi 1:6).

The fatherhood of God had deep significance for Jesus. As a lad of twelve, he remarked that his parents should not have been surprised that he was in his Father's house (Luke 2:49). He taught his disciples to pray, "Our Father" (Matthew 6:9). As the seventy returned from their successful mission, Jesus prayed joyfully: "I thank thee, 0 Father, Lord of heaven and earth" (Luke 10:21). In John 17, Jesus addressed God as "Father," "Holy Father," and "O righteous Father." On the cross he prayed, "Father, into thy hands ... " (Luke 23:46). Thomas Walter Manson, the great English New Testament scholar, reminds us that Jesus rarely spoke in public of God as Father but considered the fatherhood of God so sacred that it was reserved for his disciples who could understand. God is not the Father of men and women in general, but only of those who are trustful and obedient. Being in a personal, intimate relationship with God, Jesus could speak of God as Father. Jesus came that all persons might share this personal relationship with God the Father.

Grandchild: Can we believe that God the Father genuinely cares for us?

Granddaddy: Life teaches us very early that caring is a powerful emotion. The ability to care is reflected in various ways in our society. An attitude of tender concern is suggested by the words on the backs of some of our Christmas, birthday, or graduation cards with the slogan, "When you care enough to send the very best." It is indicated on the labels of some of the packages we mail: "handle with care." Our concern and interest in the underprivileged and homeless in foreign countries is depicted in our sending CARE packages. Sometimes our slang expression, "I couldn't care less," indicates our lack of concern and love.

This is even more important when it comes to God's care for us. The central message revealed through the incarnation is that God cares for and loves us. God could not care more! God has been disclosed through Jesus Christ as the loving Father whose love is unlimited. Although God is holy, almighty, righteous, and eternal, the inner nature of God's character has been summed up in the phrase, "God is love" (1John 4:8). The familiar words of John 3: 16 indicate the depth of God's caring.

The fatherhood of God has taken on new content in the incarnation of Jesus Christ. Through Jesus, we have seen what God is like. God is like his Son, Jesus Christ, who was kind, tender, loving, merciful, and caring. God, to the Christian, is not a "first cause" or an "unknown force" behind the universe, but is the Father of Jesus Christ. Through the Son, the Father has been focused so men and women can see God's nature of love and concern. The love of God has been expressed in the life, death, and teachings of Christ. It was eternal love in action. "He that has seen me has seen the Father" (John 14:9).

Grandchild: Who and what is God like?

Granddaddy: Jesus answered that question with his life and death. God the Father is like the Son who cares so much for his lost children that he actively seeks them out wherever they are. The parables of the lost sheep, the lost coin. and the prodigal son are word pictures that express the deep compassion and eternal vigil of God. (See Luke 15:1-32.) God is a seeking Father. whose quest is continuous because every person is precious to God (Mark 2:17; Matthew 18:11). Whether a person be lost by her own choice or by the fault or carelessness of others or through sheer neglect, God is concerned for every life, and God's seeking love calls all persons into intimate fellowship. The message of the incarnation is not that God remained coolly detached from the world but that he was involved in the world through Christ. "God was in Christ," Paul wrote in 2 Corinthians 5:19. "And the Word was made flesh and dwelt among us" (John 1:14).

Grandchild: Does God's holiness mean that God always remains hidden to us?

Granddaddy: First another story. A small boy went into a church auditorium one Sunday before the others arrived and began to look under the pews, behind the pulpit, and every place he could imagine a person to be. His mother came in and saw the youngster as he was peering behind the communion table. She asked: "What are you looking for?" "I'm looking for God," he responded. "If this is his house, why can't I find him here? Is he hiding?" The child has echoed the sentiments of many young people and adults. Why does God seem to be so far off and remote from us?

God's holiness indicates that God is uniquely different and separate from us. God, as I said earlier, is the One who is holy and "wholly" other. God is spoken of as being transcendent in recognition of the vast gulf that separates God and humanity. Since God is so radically different from us, we are unable to take the initiative in approaching God. When Moses sought to see God, he received the response: "You cannot see my face: for there shall no man see me, and live" (Exodus 33:20). God's hidden nature is derived from God's holiness, and no person is able to penetrate the mystery with his own strength.

Although God is hidden by God's holy nature, God has chosen to reveal God's self. In the "word became flesh," God has declared God's nearness to us. The way to God is not barred, for through Jesus Christ, we have access to the Father

(Ephesians 2:18; 3:12). God has come near to us, so we can approach God. God, for many, is an abstract noun, but Christ has made the abstract concrete in his person. The Word became flesh is not a concept or an idea. To Philip's question in the upper room, Jesus replied: "He that has seen me has seen the Father; and how can say you then, 'Show us the Father?'" (John 14:9).

In Christ—the Emmanuel, God with us—all persons are brought into the presence of God. Only one who was God incarnate could have revealed God to humanity. "For there is one God, and one mediator between God and men, the man Christ Jesus" (1 Timothy 2:5*)*. Frank Stagg has indicated that the title of mediator as applied to Jesus Christ means more than someone who is between God and man. "Jesus came *to overcome the betweenness* between God and man." In Jesus Christ, we have been brought into an intimate relationship with God the Father.

Grandchild: What does it mean to be called Children of God the Father?

Granddaddy: The doctrine of the fatherhood of God carries with it the idea of the children of God. Fatherhood implies sonship or daughter-ship. Although all persons have been created by God, the New Testament is quite clear in stressing that we became God's children by personal obedience to God. To become children of God, we must be born anew, born from above. (Read John 1:12-13.) No one can make himself a son or daughter of God. We become God's children by accepting the Father's invitation to enter into the divine fellowship of love. Through the name of Jesus, the personal revelation of God's nature as redeeming love has been seen. We have seen what God is like in Jesus. As the psalmist has declared: "They that know thy name will put their trust in thee" (Psalm 9:10). Those who trust in God's name have become children of God.

Jesus used an expression about God that to many Jewish minds may have appeared disrespectful. It is the word that a young child used in talking to his father. In a prayer in Mark 14:36, Jesus addressed God as "Abba Father." It is a word that is so untranslatable that the early church has preserved the original Aramaic word *Abba.* Jesus' use of this word was completely new in religious speech. The closest possible translation of the word *Abba* would probably be "Daddy' in our contemporary speech. Here Jesus speaks to his Father in the most familiar manner possible. This is an indication of an absolute and tender intimacy with God the Father. Later, this same Aramaic word, *Abba* appears in Romans 8:15 and Galatians 4:6. In these passages persons are able to address God as "Abba, Father" because he or she has become God's son or daughter through adoption. "Wherefore you are no more a servant, but a son: and if a son, then an heir of God through Christ" (Galatians 4:7). Through Jesus Christ, all persons have access to become intimate children of God. Christ has revealed God's nature as redemptive love and has opened up for us a relationship with the Father that can be best described as a Father-son/daughter relation.

Consider again the question, What's in a name? This depends upon who bears the name. Some children have not had a good father image. We might need to consider what image we might use to convey to a young person what God is like, when the only earthly father that person has ever known is a drunkard. If the only father image a young person has is a lazy, uncaring, irresponsible drug addict, it will be difficult for him or her to have a clear understanding of the fatherhood of God. The book, *God Is for Real, Man* by Carl F. Burke might provide some helpful suggestions for further discussion along this line. We will need to remind them that God is like the loving God revealed in the sacrificial love of Jesus Christ who reaches out tenderly to all persons with divine love.

An image of God

Grandchild: I wonder sometimes if God is playing hide and seek with us. It is hard to get a clear image of God's presence.

Granddaddy: Images play an important role in our society today. Certain images determine styles, mannerisms, tastes, and preferences. The advertising market is well aware that images influence what people buy, eat, and wear, as well as where they go, stay, and play. All these images have influenced our image of God as well. Young people do often have strange images of God. Sometimes their image of God is fuzzy and distorted, but an image is there. Sometimes it is influenced by concepts that are childish and immature, but the desire to know what God's nature is like is real and genuine. What is essential, then, is a proper image of God. The true image of God is revealed in Jesus Christ, and in him the nature of God and man is clarified.

Grandchild: Where can we begin to get a valid image of God?

Granddaddy: The desire to know what God's nature is like is an ultimate question. Individuals have raised it in the midst of their suffering, in the darkness of their own night, and in the feeling of their absolute· aloneness. It is a question that demands, rather that pleads for, a clear image of God. Many centuries ago, the prophet Isaiah raised the penetrating inquiry: "To whom then will you liken God? or what likeness will you compare unto him?" (Isaiah 40:18).

Where do we begin in trying to make a comparison? We usually project from our own nature what we conceive God to be like. We have purposed that in some way God is like us. Of course, this is anthropomorphism (attributing human qualities to God), but we can think in no other images or analogies. This does not imply that God has a bodily form and walks in the fields and listens with physical ears. This is a primitive view arising from a crude form of anthropomorphism. The highest and best characteristics found in humanity, however, are surely a clue to the nature of God. Jesus interpreted God in human terms when he compared human fatherhood to divine fatherhood (Matthew 7:11).

In the Bible, God is not seen as an abstract force or an unknown cause, God is assumed to be a personal God. When reference is made to God, God is addressed as "Thou," and God speaks as "I." (See Exodus 3:14; Psalms 23:4; 83:18; 113:28; Lamentations 5:19; Isaiah 41:4; Matthew 26:39). To say that God is holy, just, loving, and righteous is to ascribe qualities that are only appropriate to a personal being. Since only persons can make moral choices, God's moral character presupposes that God is personal. God's personal nature is implied throughout the Bible in terms of man's trust, dependence, fellowship, forgiveness, and guidance. The phrase, "Our Father," could be addressed only to a personal God. Although God may be conceived after the analogy of human beings, God is always so much greater than our thoughts about God (Isaiah 40:28). Nevertheless, we are aware of an intimate fellowship with the divine. The apostle Paul has expressed it well: "For I know whom I have believed, and am persuaded that he is able to keep that which I have committed unto him against that day" (2 Timothy 1:12).

God, male or female

Grandchild: I heard an eight-year-old girl ask her pastor if God likes boys better than girls. She believes that God is a boy, therefore he must favor boys. Is God male or female, both or neither? What does this question imply about God's nature? I guess what I am asking is: what is the nature of God? Is God like a person?

Granddaddy: Although God is often depicted in the Bible as though God is male, I personally do not believe that sexual images are appropriate to describe God. God is neither male or female, yet incorporates both, nevertheless is not limited by these images. These images are our human projections on God. God cannot be limited by maleness or femaleness. God's nature as Spirit is personal, but that does not mean that God is "a" person. God transcends all human depictions and human projections.

In the revelation of God as recorded in the New Testament, there is a new divine image. The new image of God is the one made known in Jesus Christ. The writer of the book of Hebrews begins his epistle with a reference to the various ways God has spoken to humanity in the past, and then he focuses on the revelation in Christ. He describes the relationship of Jesus to his Father as "the express image of his person" (Hebrews 1:3). If anyone wants to understand God's nature, let her begin with Jesus. Study his life, his teachings, his death, and learn what his risen presence meant to the early church and what it denotes for us today. The face of God has been revealed through the person of Christ.

The incarnation of God in Jesus Christ is the central emphasis of the Christian faith. The revelation of God's personal nature has been made clear in "the Word was made flesh." In the incarnation of the *Word,* God's revelation has become uniquely personal and historical. Since man/woman is a person, he or she can understand fully only that which is personal, and since God is a personal being, God reveals God's self in a personal way. The revelation which the Bible affirms about God is not of an object to a subject, but from subject to subject. Revelation is not concerned with giving information about God, but with the personal encounter and personal communion persons can have with the living God.

The personal nature of God's revelation is made clear in the Gospel of John by the concept of the *Word* (John 1:4). Far from being an abstract or impersonal term, the Word describes the personal incarnation of God within history in Jesus Christ. Knowledge about a person is not the same as knowing that individual personally. Someone may say that he knows something *about* God; but this is not the same as declaring that he knows God *personally.*

A person reads that "God is love," but the truth of this statement will not be fully realized until God has been experienced as love. Jesus Christ has unveiled God's eternal love within the world. In him is seen the fulness of God's love. Apart from the personal revelation of God in Christ, the terms, "God is love" and "Jesus is Lord," have little or no meaning (John 3:16; 2 John 7-10). The meaning is given in and with the event itself. They are not static ideas that can be arrived at by scientific methods, but he becomes Lord to a man only when that individual commits his or her life in trust to Christ, having been led by the spirit of God to the one who is the truth.

   *Meaning in life*

Grandchild: How are we to understand who we are as human beings? What and who are we really as persons?

Granddaddy: Who is this creature called man/woman? The question of the psalmist is echoed through the centuries. "What is man, that thou art mindful of him?" (Psalm 8:4). Who and what is this man/woman? Is the ballad correct? "How many roads must a man walk down, before they call him a man? ... The answer ... is written in the wind." Is it? Is it not, instead, written in the revelation of the incarnate Christ? In Christ, the interaction of divine and human are revealed in the One who is "both very God and very man." Christ has not only revealed to us something about God's nature, but ours as well. Some people have been content to depict man/woman as an animal and no more. Others see human beings as a complicated machine, while another describes us as an accident of fate whose life is without purpose or meaning. On the other hand, the biblical picture of humanity presents us as a creature who has been created in the image of God. (Genesis 1:26-27; 1 Corinthians 11:7). The creation of the image of God within us was God's way of endowing us with some measure of God's own personal nature. The fact that we have been created in the image of God is the reason it is possible for us to have communion with God. H. Wheeler Robinson, an Old Testament scholar, states: "Whatever the doubtful phrase, 'the image of God,' may mean, it is certainly intended to recognize man's unique relation to God, and his supremacy over the animal world." God's revelation is not given to an inanimate object but to persons. It is person-to-person. Man/woman is what he or she is because God created us that way. We are different from dirt, animals, and plants because we were created to have fellowship with God.

God has given to us the gift of self-conscious reason. This is true of human beings alone. We share in the nature of God by God's creative act. The coming of the "Word ... made flesh" indicates the supreme worth God maintains for God's creation. If we were not significant to God, the incarnation would not have happened. Maybe this is the reason some people still reject the fact today. Their opinion of humanity is too low. God's grace and love indicate the lengths to which God will go to bring us back into divine fellowship. Since God has revealed the worth God feels for us, we need to have respect for our own worth and the worthiness of others. No person should ever be treated as an object or a thing. No person is an "it," but a person who was created in God's image. Our sin may have marred the image, but it is not destroyed. That "image" is the point of contact for God's ever-seeking spirit. We were created to commune with God and we will be restless until we rest in God.

Grandchild: Is it possible for us as believers to communicate this divine image to others?

Granddaddy: The wonder of the Christian gospel is that God's nature was disclosed through a life lived among us. The image of God was plowed into history in Jesus Christ. The gospel was not first flashed on a television or movie screen, or read in a book or newspaper, it was seen and known in a personal life—in the life of Christ. The faith of the disciples, John declared, was founded upon this personal life. (Read 1 John 1:1-2.) Just as the gospel came through Christ, so it is to be translated through other lives. "You shall be witnesses unto me," Jesus told those who followed him. From generation to generation, men and women have given witness to the effect of Christ on their lives, and these individuals in turn have passed on through their lives the gospel to others.

In Romans 2:16, Paul uses the phrase *"my* gospel." At the first reading this strikes a strange note. Should it not be *"the* gospel"? But there is a gospel according to each of us. We bear witness to it every day *in and through our lives.* We write a gospel of some kind every day, and it will be read. The sound, the style, the type, and the lines of the gospel according to us may not be Christian, but it will be read and heard. Through our lives, the gospel of Christ is either being revealed as he would have us reveal it, or it is being distorted. God works through persons to reveal God's character. The Word becomes flesh in Christ, and the One who is our eternal Contemporary must become real in us.

As the power of Christ enters our lives, we become responsible for translating the image of Christ through our lives to others. Paul says of the Christian that each person, whether he or she admits it or not, is an advertisement or a reference for Christ. Listen to him! "Do we need, as some apparently do, to exchange testimonials before we can be friends? You yourselves are our testimonial, written in our hearts and yet open for anyone to inspect and read. You are an open letter about Christ which we ourselves have written, not with pen and ink but with the Spirit of the living God. Our message has been engraved, not in stone but in living men and women" (2 Corinthians 3:1-3, Phillips).

I believe that personality is the highest reality of which persons are aware, both within one's self and in God. God's revelation, especially the disclosure in Jesus Christ, has indicated that God deals with us in a personal way. The image of God in us is the divine stamp of personhood upon each individual. Every personality is sacred to God and demands one's own self-respect and proper regard for the worth of others. We are never to treat others less than human beings. God's nature as personal love has been made known through the person of Christ. Christ's continued presence is seen in and through the lives of Christians today. The One who is uniquely personal seeks to work through the personal lives of his disciples in the world today.

Loving hateful people

Grandchild: How can we possibly love people who are hateful to us or even be nice to them? Are we really supposed to behave that way?

Granddaddy: You are right. That is a difficult thing to do. Jesus taught us that we are to "love our enemies" as recorded in Matthew 5:43-44. But that seems like something that is not only difficult but impossible to do. We sometimes say we should hate the sin but love the sinner. That seems like a silly, straw-splitting distinction until we reflect that we do that with ourselves. We do things all the time that we do not think are right and forgive ourselves for doing them and keep on loving ourselves. C. S. Lewis, the English writer, reminds us that the love we are called to direct toward our enemies in loving and forgiving them is not an emotional love but based on the *Agape* Christian love that arises not from emotions, goose bumps or feelings. This kind of love is an effort of the will and not our emotions. We seek to respond to others as we want them to respond to us. As Jesus said, "Do unto others as you would have them do to you." This kind of love, according to Lewis, means that we do not have to like a person to exercise *Agape* love. We strive to distinguish between a person and his or her actions, and endeavor to hate things and not the person, and to forgive as we know God has forgiven us for our own sins. Recognizing that this is not easy, we attempt to direct our will to respond to criticism with an ear for learning, words of accusation with self-control, unjust condemnation with humility, and anger with patience. This is never easy, but I think it is the Christ-like way. I can't pretend that I always succeed in doing this, but I do believe it is the Christian way of *agape* love. Responding negatively and in an ugly manner to those who criticize us, is a road to disaster, rejection, and self-defeat.

Grandchild: Does that mean we simply excuse their sinfulness?

Granddaddy. No. This does not mean that we simply ignore a person's bad behavior or dismiss their hateful actions. People need to know they have to be accountable to God and others for their behavior and seek to find ways to live honorably with others. We do not condone their sin or misbehavior, but strive to guide and assist them in finding forgiveness and the path to amend their wrong deeds or actions. Hopefully, as they discover the forgiving love of God and our forgiveness, they can learn to live meaningful and ethical lives.

Depression

Grandchild: Sometimes I feel a little depressed. Is that normal or bad? I have friends here at college that often speak about being depressed.

Granddaddy: No one is immune from depression. All of us will feel low at some time in our lives. I think that is normal. Depression is indeed a big problem on college campuses with young people today. We can't be on the mountaintop of high emotions all the time. Many factors can cause depression, even in young people. It can be the attitudes of peers toward you, illness, grief experiences, loneliness, failure in school, rejection by a boyfriend or girlfriend, conflicts with parents, low self-esteem, image issues, or many other factors. Don't let your low moods determine your perspective in life. When depressed, talk to someone who can help you and will listen -- a close friend, a parent, grandparent, your minister, or counselor. Find ways to get involved in doing something to help others through your church group, school, scouts, or some other organization. Reach back on your inner spiritual resources that give us the assurance that God is always available to strengthen us and is present with God's abiding presence in all circumstances. We will never escape all the problems and difficulties of life, but, as Christians, we seek to trust in Christ to "walk" with us through all situations.

Suicide

Grandchild: I have a friend who has talked with me about her feelings of wanting to commit suicide. How do I respond to her?

Granddaddy: Oh, goodness. Suicide is a major problem in our country and around the world. Many thousands of people take their lives every year. I think it is getting worse every year. There are many reasons young people take their lives—bullying, depression, a sense of futility, illness, accidents, grief, guilt, a sense of disgrace, failure, or many other causes. I would encourage you to listen with compassion and wise sensitivity to your friend; encourage her to find counseling with a professional counselor or a minister, to talk with her parents, if she can; express your love and support; assist her to find a support group to help her get through this dark period; and reassure her that she can call you or text you when she has these low feelings and needs your support. Remind her that she is never alone but God is always with her and wants to love and strengthen her even when she cannot feel or sense that divine Presence.

The will of God

Grandchild: How can we know the will of God for our lives?

Granddaddy: I wish I could tell you that there is a simple answer for that question. But I have not found it easy to determine God's guidance for *my* life. I have often wished that I could pick up my phone and dial direct or send a text and say: "Hello God, this is Bill. I have a problem. Would you please tell me what to do?" But I can't honestly say that I have had a phone call from God or a text message. No audible voice told me what I should do. Neither have I had visions in the night instructing me on what I was supposed to do. To be honest, I am not comfortable with those persons who claim that they have had such experiences.

Some turn to strange places to get guidance for the future. They use Ouija boards, crystal balls, fortune tellers, tea leaves, cards, horoscopes, and astrologists, or seek to find directions from the stars. Don't trust those phony connivers. Where do we go for guidance in making decisions for life? There is no machine called "Divine Guidance" with instructions reading: "Put your question in the slot, push it in, and out will come the divine answer." I wish knowing God's will was that simple, but it isn't.

I have found several things helpful for me in seeking God's guidance for my life. I believe God expects us to use the reasoning powers God created us to have. Apprise the situation before you and determine with your best reasoning powers what you think is the best direction or choice to make. Study the Scriptures and seek to discern what you believe is the way Jesus made his decisions. Before you decide, ask yourself if this approach seems in keeping with the way of Christ. Through regular worship and Bible study, Christ's way can become clearer to you. Then seek to follow in that way. If a decision is knowingly dishonest, immoral, unethical, or harmful to another, you know that is not the will of God for you.

Follow the light you already have. As I have walked in the light I already have, I have found that further light was cast on the road ahead of me. We walk in faith and trust and never have absolute clarity. At least that has been my discovery. It requires patience and the ability to "wait" on the Lord for further light. I have often discovered that I have never fully known God's will except in retrospect—looking back God's will has become clearer. We walk in faith not with complete sight.

Grandchild: How can we find meaning in life? There are so many voices pulling at us telling us they have the answer. What is the Christian response?

Granddaddy: I believe that the real meaning in life is found only in dedication to something outside of oneself with such intense commitment that one forgets about one's self. Life's motto cannot read "safety first" if one is to achieve the higher happiness. The *old* maxim reads: "Self-preservation is nature's first law." Well, if that is true, Jesus has given us a higher law in his paradoxical statement: "Whosoever will save his life shall lose it: but whosoever will lose his life for my sake, the same shall save it" (Luke 9:24).

Is it possible that we save ourselves only in spending ourselves? A closer examination of life reveals that this is true. If a student tries to save his mind by not using it until he goes to college, he discovers that he is the loser. He learns only by using his mind, not by ceasing to study. No person can save her body by not using it. The physical body which is exercised remains healthy. By using her muscles, a person can keep them strong. Failure to exercise results in a flabby body and weak muscles. A pianist develops his skill only by practice and playing. Without spending considerable time in practice, he loses his proficiency. The paradox is true: We save only by spending ourselves, receive only by giving, and find only by losing.

The noted Austrian psychiatrist Viktor Frankl has observed that a boomerang is not designed primarily to come back to the thrower. It returns to the thrower only when he has missed the target. The focus on self-interest, I believe, reveals that we have missed the purpose and meaning in life. Frankl's conviction is that a person finds meaning in life only "to the extent to which he commits himself to something beyond himself, to a cause greater than himself." Frankl's own harrowing years in Auschwitz, the grim German concentration camp, reveal his own search for "a will to meaning." During his agonizing experience he concluded that if a man has a "why" for living, he can endure almost any "how." Without something to live *for* man will be unable to sense what life is all *about*.

The Christian finds the "why" to life's meaning beyond one's self in the call to discipleship and in commitment to the living Christ. External happiness, if it comes, is a by-product and is not deliberately sought. Commit yourself to some cause, purpose, goal that seeks to make life better for others; challenge some wrong or difficulty others are experiencing; enlighten others; lift up the abused, hurting, weak, or neglected persons; wage a battle against war and evil, injustice, and political corruption; share the Good News of Christ with others; educate children and youth; strive to overcome poverty, disease, racism, pollution, prejudice; endeavor for a goal that will make life better for others and do not seek primarily personal recognition for yourself.

A closed fist is unable to receive. The Dead Sea remains dead because it has no outlet. A life spent only on self is a dead life. The overflowing life is the abundant life, while the selfish life can only end in stagnation. It is sometimes difficult to make a living, but it is so much harder to make a life. Life has meaning for those who have linked their lives with a cause and a purpose bigger than they are. The Christian is called to link his or her life with the Kingdom of God and to engage in the quest to fulfil it "on earth as it is in heaven." Instead, give first place to his Kingdom and to what he requires, and he will provide you with all these other things" (Matthew 6:33, TEV).

Responding to BS

Grandchild: Why do politicians and prominent leaders often tell so many lies, make false claims, and assert so much BS?

Granddaddy: That is indeed a good question, and unfortunately too true. Some political leaders, and even renowned world leaders, including some religious figures, have made so many obviously untrue or false claims or pronouncements that it calls into question their truthfulness and character. I read a book recently by a Princeton philosophy professor who had written a book titled *On BullS---*. He asserted the lack of stability, the skeptical dissolution, the lack of any significant connection between a person's opinions and his or her apprehensions of reality, the absence of any moral agent, disinterest in determining truth or falsehood, deceptive misrepresentation, and many other factors as "BS" which is a genuine cause for critical concern about the welfare of our country and an honest sense of truthfulness. It is a real problem in our society today. We used to hear people say, "my word is my bond." You could trust what they said or did. Lying, being dishonest, untruthful, and making up things to get one's way or to make a point—BS…ing – is not the Christian or moral approach to life. If we lose our sense of character or moral campus, we will go down a road to ethical chaos and immoral behavior. Seek the high road through life that strives to model itself after the Christ-like way that leads to the highest character and moral standards one can reach for.

   *Drugs and alcohol*

Grandchild: On many college campuses today, drugs and alcohol are a huge problem for those of us who are college students. How do we try to live in an environment that is so inundated with these temptations?

Granddaddy: I agree. Drugs and drinking are a bigger problem than ever today. A part of the problem stems from the fact that we live in a society that advocates using pills, stimulants, sedatives, "uppers" and "downers" to help us sleep or to assist us to get up in the morning. Amphetamines, barbiturates, and tranquilizers are consumed by the billions in what is called a normal or prescribed usage. Many homes use alcohol in many forms to an excess that telegraphs to their children that excessive drinking is OK. Drug abuse from marijuana, cocaine, heroin, LSD to opioid addiction has spanned the decades. Some students have learned to abuse such amphetamines as Benzedrine, Dexedrine, and Methergine as well as certain sedatives. Narcotics or opiates have hooked many a young person. College binge parties have often led to destructive behavior in too many young people's lives. They often start out with what appears to be just a minor drug that offers merely a "little" high, and soon they are hooked on more addictive drugs.

All of this is a real challenge for a Christian young person, especially those in college. I would encourage you to build a strong support group with friends you make in your church groups or campus religious organizations. Avoid frat parties and other occasions that thrust you with those who want to do heavy drinking or abuse drugs. As you are striving to become a mature adult, realize that you will always need your best mental faculties and moral determination to make the best and sane decision in your life. Hold on to what you know is the highest and best moral standards you have learned in your Christian teachings, and be willing to say,

"No," without fear of not being accepted. This will not always be easy, but, I believe, you will be a stronger person for learning to resist these kinds of temptations.

Christians and cursing

Grandchild: Are expletives that we as Christian chose to say sinful, or does it say in the Bible that curse words are sinful?

Granddaddy: Cursing or the use of profanity is so wide spread in our society today through movies, television, and casual conversation that many are beginning to think that it is acceptable at any time or place. There is no question, in my opinion, that there are occasions where a damn a hell or some other expletive might be an appropriate response. Used rarely and in an appropriate time and place is different from one whose vocabulary is constantly filled with profane words. I honestly believe that for a person to fill his or her conversation with profanity, especially the F-bomb -- is an indication of a lack of a strong vocabulary, a lack of control, a lack of maturity, and may even be a reflection on their level of intelligence. I have tried to guard my speech to avoid using profanity except in rare times when the "situation" seems to require it. Jesus reminds us that what comes out of our mouth is a reflection of what is in our heart (Matthew 15:17-20). The Bible also instructs us to remember to "Set a guard over my mouth, O Lord. Keep watch over the door of my lips (Psalm 141:3) and "Let the words of my mouth and the meditation of my heart be acceptable to you, O Lord, my rock and my redeemer" (Psalm 19:14). I think it is a poor reflection on one who claims to be a Christian and who is at the same time constantly using profanity in one's conversation. That in my opinion is sinful behavior. Always strive to let your speech be a reflection of the quality of your character.

Casual sex

Grandchild: Is engaging in what is called casual sex wrong?

Granddaddy: I know that casual sex or "hooking up," as young people like to describe it today, is a frequent occurrence. I personally think that one should reserve one's sexual commitment for the person you really love and want to share your life with in the bond of marriage. Casual sex cheapens the beautiful relationship one should want to share with the person you deeply love. Casual sex also exposes one to the dangers of various venereal diseases and even AIDS. No one should try to force another person to "show" them their affection by participating in sex. This is not a revelation of love but an attempt to coerce another person to yield to their control. That is not love but coercion. I believe that God designed sex to be that beautiful bond that helps unite two loving people in a spiritual as well as a physical relationship. Sex, therefore, was not created to be a causal relationship but one of a deep and lasting commitment. I look forward to the day you can make a lasting bond with the one you love and want to spend the rest of your life with.

Racial and sexual orientation

Grandchild: If God is loving and accepting of all, then why do some people of the church congregation not accept others of different races or sexual orientation? Why do some say that being gay is a sin?

Granddaddy: That is a challenging question. Unfortunately, many in our church congregations have either not accepted or understood the teachings of Jesus about the unconditional nature of

God's love. The New Testament shows Jesus reaching out to persons in all walks of life—the poor and rich, lepers (unclean people by Jewish law) and Samaritans (despised people by the Jews then), the irreligious and the tax collectors (again despised by the Jews then), a woman caught in the act of adultery, non-Jewish foreigners from another country, talking to a Samaritan woman by a well at noon-time, and many other references --to confirm how Jesus reached across racial, cultural and religious lines to demonstrate the love and openness of God's grace to all persons. In the favorite verse of most Christians in John 3: 16, we are told that "God so loved the world—the whole world—that God gave His only begotten son" for our redemption. That **"all"** includes persons of all races, classes, nationalities, sexual orientation, etc. who believe in Christ. **ALL!** In the Book of Acts, one of the first Christian converts is an Ethiopian eunuch (Acts 8:26-40).

Now I know that some try to focus on selected Scripture verses like 1 Corinthians 6:9, 1 Timothy 1:10 and Romans 1:28-32 to "prove" that homosexuality is an unforgivable sin. The major problem with this isolated reading is the fact that many Greek scholars note that the Greek word translated as homosexual in these passages is a word that Paul seems to have "coined" for these letters to address the sexual immorality and bad behavior problems occurring in the early church. Some have proposed that a better rendering of this rare word might be sexual exploiters, rapists, sexual predators, or pimps. Paul was concerned with all the sexual "looseness" that was transpiring in the church along with drunkards, idolaters, thieves, greedy, revilers, robbers, etc. Do we likewise condemn these persons to hell without the possibility of forgiveness? In the very next verse, Paul indicates these sins were what used to be the nature of the persons to whom he is writing, but God has justified them in Christ Jesus (6:11).

The attempt to make homosexuality a sin denies the reality that being gay is not a choice one makes, but is the way one is born. Scientists indicate it is genetic. To try to get a gay person to undergo what is called "ex-gay therapy" is to declare that something is not right with him or her, and he or she needs to change. Studies have shown that the so called "ex-gay therapy" does not work, because a person cannot change how he or she was born. LGBTQ persons are God's children, like the rest of us, and the church needs to recognize this and acknowledge that they can experience God's love, grace, and forgiveness like everyone else can. In one of my churches I was called to the hospital to minister to a member who was dying with AIDS. He asked me if he had committed the unpardonable sin. I assured him that he had not, and that God loved him unconditionally. After he died, at his funeral, I conducted the memorial service for one, I believed, who had died in the faith, trusting in the love and grace of God.

If a church congregation is going to follow the teachings of Jesus, then it needs to be open to all persons as Christ was and is. To be honest, all of us are still prejudice in many ways, and we have to continue working to overcome this attitude. The church is charged with continuing to confront, educate, and guide its disciples in the loving sacrificial path Christ would have us follow. The small letter of John reminds us, "Those who say, 'I love God,' and hate their brothers or sisters, are liars; for those who do not love a brother or sister whom they have seen, cannot love God whom they have not seen. The commandment we have from him is this: those who love God must love their brothers and sisters also" (1John 4:20-21).

Loving one's neighbor

Grandchild: If the church is supposed to be "loving thy neighbor as thyself," why is there so much disconnect between churches and its congregations?

Granddaddy: That question reflects, unfortunately, the kinds of conflicts, racism, prejudice, discord, dogmatism, arrogance, and various issues that have plagued the church through the ages and into our contemporary scene today. This disconnect reveals how far the local and world-wide church must go to follow the teaching of

Jesus to love our neighbor as our self. This disconnect exists because the members in many congregations are divided into "camps" or groups based on their prejudice, dogmatism, ignorance, selfishness, arrogance, desire to control, etc. rather than seeking to find the Christ-like way of love and concern for one's brother or sister in Christ. Many have not acknowledged that we can't speak of loving God without loving our neighbor.

Jesus said that the first and greatest commandment of all the commandments was that you love the Lord your God with your total being. He said that the second was like unto the first. "You shall love your neighbor as yourself" is like unto the first and greatest commandment. In what way is there a likeness? There is a likeness in the sense that both of these commandments are intertwined. You really can't talk about loving God and not loving your neighbor. You can't claim to love God and hate someone who is nearby. Jesus combines these two, because love ultimately comes from God. We love because God first loved us (1 John 4:19). The hand might serve as an analogy. Both sides of the hand, the top and bottom, constitute the hand. Each is a part of the whole. If there is going to be genuine love both sides are essential. You can't talk about loving God in the abstract, without at the same time loving human beings that you are around all the time. These two commandments are like two sides of the same coin. They cannot be separated. Love of God and human beings are bound together.

This does not mean that we always have to like our neighbor or the things he or she does. This Christian act of love is not based on emotions or feelings but is *Agape* love which means that it is an act of the will. I exercise *Agape* love because it seeks to love another as I would want that person to love me. Remembering Jesus' word, "Do unto others as you would have them do to you." As long as selfishness, arrogant behavior, or a dictatorial attitude prevails in churches, the command from Jesus, to love your neighbor as yourself, will not become a reality. James reminds us in his small epistle that "Faith without works is dead" (James 2:20). We can talk about having religion, but it is real only when there is evidence in our behavior and actions. I believe Jesus wants his church to be open, loving, accepting of all persons of all races and colors or sexual orientation, and always striving to support and love one another, bearing one another's burdens, comforting the sick and grieving, helping the poor and needy, guiding the younger, weaker, or newer Christian brother or sister in the way of Jesus, teaching one another the Gospel of Christ and how one might share that message of universal love and grace with others.

The church, if it is to be the church Jesus founded, must be built on love. Helmut Thielicke, the German theologian, has offered a suggestion that we should turn the lawyer's question around. We do not need to ask, "Who is my neighbor," as the Pharisee asked. Our question should be, "To whom am *I* a neighbor?" Human concerns and needs are all around us in our churches and in our neighborhoods. How can we be a neighbor? Jesus has told us that the commandment to love our neighbor as ourselves is like the one about loving God. When you and I, as members of Christ's church, "Love your neighbor as yourself," this disconnect, you speak of, I believe, will be resolved. We obviously are not there yet. May Christ help us to get there.

Forgiveness for murderers and terrorists

Grandchild: Does God forgive murderers and those who bring terror to other individuals?

Granddaddy: That's a tough question. But I believe the New Testament teaches us that God does forgive these persons. Hang with me now. One example is when Jesus is dying on the cross and the thief or murderer on one side of Jesus' cross, who was also being crucified, asked Jesus to remember him when he came into his kingdom. Jesus tells him that "This day you will be with me in paradise." But for God to forgive such awful murderers like Hitler in World War II, the nine-eleven terrorist attack on the Twin Towers, the murder of the nine-innocent people in the prayer service in the Emanuel African Methodist Episcopal Church in Charleston, SC, the death of the twenty innocent children and six teachers and staff at Sandy Hook, Newtown, CT, and the many suicide bombings of terrorists today demands consequences also. I believe this is where an understanding of hell comes in. These people must first enter hell after death to experience the purging, redeeming, purifying power of God's remedial grace. People who have committed grievous acts are far removed from what God desires his creative children to be like. They must undergo teaching, guiding, directing, and learning on a spiritual track moving them toward understanding what genuine, authentic living is.

Who knows how long this process may take? If one begins in the next life where one leaves off here, murderers and terrorists have a long way to go in reaching spiritual maturity. If God is love, I believe, that God will never rest in seeking to convert these persons to be the authentic persons God has created them to be. The Apostle's Creed declares that "Jesus descended into hell." Why? I believe it was to seek to bring redemption to these "lost" persons there. Is this what 1 Peter 3:18-19 and 4:6 are suggesting? The noted theologian Walter Rauschenbusch declared that God could not rejoice at anyone being in hell. He asserted that Christ would lead an invasion into hell itself to recover the one lost sheep of his ninety- nine saved ones. I believe hell is not God's vindictive way to punish individuals, but rather hell is educational and redemptive. If God's love and mercy are unconditional, then, I believe, this must be true.

Being as forgiving as Jesus

Grandchild: How can we, as Christians, be as forgiving as Jesus?

Granddaddy: To be honest, I don't think we can be as forgiving as Jesus, because he was God's Son and we are human. That does not mean we should not attempt to be as forgiving as Jesus. He is our model and guide for forgiveness. In the model prayer, Jesus taught his disciples, as we are charged to pray: "Forgive us our wrongs as we have forgiven those who have wronged us" (Matthew 6:12, *The New English Bible*). Our forgiveness by God is tempered by the way we forgive others. Being unwilling to forgive others, I think, blocks our ability to accept God's forgiveness of ourselves. We cannot deny our own sinfulness and the necessity of asking God for forgiveness.

When Peter asked Jesus how many times we should forgive others, he wondered if it was up to seven times. Jesus responded by saying it should be seventy times seven. By this, I think he meant, our forgiveness of others should be endless. He stressed that his disciples are to turn the other cheek; go the second mile; give the coat off your back to another. These teachings call us to a higher way of forgiveness to be like Jesus. Having experience God's love and forgiving grace, we must not harbor any hidden chamber of hatred toward another person, but seek to open our spirit to the forgiving Spirit of God which we ourselves have experienced. Learning how to forgive like Jesus is a life-time journey which summons us to follow in his teachings and steps.

Significance of prayer

Grandchild: Can God help turn us away from sin, if we pray? How come it feels sometimes like prayer works well, and sometimes if doesn't?

Granddaddy: The Scriptures assure us that when we face temptations that we are not left alone. We can draw strength from the presence of God who is available to us through prayer. Paul wrote "I can do all things through Christ who strengthens me" (Philippians 4:13). In his letter to the Corinthians, Paul declares "No temptation has overtaken you that is not common to man (or woman). God is faithful, and he will not let you be tempted beyond your strength, but with the temptation will also provide the way of escape that you may be able to endure it" (1 Corinthians 10:13). Every temptation provides us an opportunity to choose. If we choose evil ways, we can crush ourselves against the moral and spiritual laws of God. I have never had God's voice shout loudly to me or flash a visible warning sign, but I have had a strong inner prayerful sense at times that the choice challenging me to turn in their direction was clearly not following the teachings of Christ or would lead me down a path that I realize was not morally or ethically right.

Prayer is not a magical wand to ward off temptations or a means to get what we may want, but rather is a means of sensing the Presence and direction of God. It is true that sometimes we feel that we have had our prayer answered, and at other times not. Jesus has encouraged us to keep on seeking, to keep on asking, to keep on praying. Whether we sense it or not, I believe that God is still responding to us, sometimes in a way we may least expect. Even Jesus, as he faced the cross, did not get the response to avoid death of the cross, but he yielded to his Father's will.

Ultimately, all us have to pray that whatever we are praying for is within God's will. Everything we often pray for, if we are honest, may be what we really desire but may not be in accordance with God's will for our lives. The very fact that we will seek to pray before making a puzzling or alluring decision, is assurance that we are really trying to discern God's will in the situation. In Matthew 6:13 Jesus taught us to seek God's strength not to be tempted to follow the path of evil when the times of testing come. I do indeed believe praying affords us inner resources to resist temptations. And I believe that God always answers our prayers, but not always in the way we ask or may desire. Sometimes God also may be saying, "No" to us, or "Wait."

Not losing hope

Grandchild: During times of struggle and hardships, why isn't praying enough? An example of what I'm asking is, if someone has cancer and we pray and pray every day for a cure and that they will survive, why doesn't it work sometimes? Why do people die when we pray for so much hope?

Granddaddy: That is indeed one of the really hard questions for Christians to confront. Through my many years as pastor, I have seen numerous people pray for loved ones and friends that they might be cured of some dread disease, only to see them die. On the other hand, I have witnessed some people get well after much prayer. What made the difference? I frankly don't know. All the people who prayed were faithful church people; and they did not all receive the same response. I think we have to begin with the understanding that prayer is not magic, nor does God promise that all our prayers will be answered just like we pray them. God has created the world where the possibility of disease, accidents, disasters, tragedies, etc. are real possibilities. None of us is immune from them. They are a part of the natural order of things, and expecting God to change them at our wish, could create havoc in our world.

Suppose we could change anything we did not like with a prayer. What kind of universe would we live in? I mentioned earlier that God has created a world that is orderly, and we must seek to live in accordance with that principle. Prayer is not an effort to change God's mind as it is more of an effort to align our mind with God's mind and will. Prayer should be our approach to be attuned to God and what God wants for us, not how we might persuade God to do something different. Why cancer or any disease is a part of our natural world, I do not really understand. I do not think we are going against God's will when we strive to find cures for such or eradicate them. Suffering is a natural part of life, and we should expect it, learn from it, overcome it, if we can, but should not offer simple answers to the profound question of "Why?"

During any person's pain, suffering, agony or whatever, I believe that God is there. God is always present in good and difficult times. We can have the assurance that no matter how difficult life might be for any of us, family, or friends—everyone--God is closer than breath itself. Archbishop Desmond Tutu reminds us that "the path to joy, like sadness, did not lead away from suffering and adversity but through it… Nothing beautiful comes without some suffering." But God is always with us-- in the good and bad times, and always teaching us. I believe we must continue to pray for those who suffer from cancer or other diseases, and we may not have answers to our questions of why they do not get well. I do believe, however, that we may not have the answers to our questions, but the **Answerer**, God, is always present with the sufferer and with those who are praying as well. Our goal is to seek to be in God's presence and to know his will for us. It may only be in the next life that we can ask God for clear answers to such puzzling questions and concerns.

The death of loved ones

Grandchild: Why does God take away some of the ones we love away from us so soon?

Granddaddy: My first response is to state that I do not think God personally sends cancer or some disease or an accident to a person to take that person's life. As I said earlier, God has created a world where these kinds of things can happen, but I do not believe God picks out a person and says, "This is the one I want to die young." Illness, suffering, bad coincidences can happen to any of us at any age, and it is not because God handpicked a particular person to suffer or die. The question, however, still remains, why do some die young or unexpectedly? Again, there is no easy answer. Maybe these persons, unfortunately early in their lives, were exposed to some germs; had inherited some physical weakness; were born with defective genes; inadequate immune system; encountered some unexpected dilemma or accident or had some other factor that caused their illness or early death. God does not interfere with the natural happenings in the created world. It is always sad when one dies young but let us not assume that is what God desires. I think God is sad, too. God, I believe, is "suffering" with us. God wants the best for all of us, but for some reason, these tragic things do happen. This is another one of those issues, I place in a mental drawer awaiting further light from God.

Grandchild: When we turn to God in times of need and still feel in need of help, how can we refrain from losing hope?

Granddaddy: All of us at some time in our lives may feel like we have hit bottom and that we are alone and without hope. Dark moments may come into our lives when we feel we have been misunderstood, rejected, belittled, criticized, failed, been hurt, lost a job, experienced a romantic breakup or many other factors. Whether we allow the darkness of the mood to overwhelm us or seek some light to bear us through the darkness is critical. We are faced with a choice: do we surrender to the attitude of despair and cynicism or choose instead the path of faith and hope? Either choice requires a commitment. Not choosing is choosing the way of defeat. We are faced with choosing to hope or despair. I think we choose to believe in hope and not despair as Christians. We may not fully understand why we are in the "slough of despondency" at this moment in our lives, but we do not give in to defeat or despair because we know we do not face this moment alone. Christ, our Lord, is present to comfort, guide us, and sustain us. We affirm with the psalmist, "The Lord is my shepherd and I shall not want." And with Paul, we affirm: "I can do all things through Christ." Whatever difficulty you face, be assured you are never alone. Christ is with you seeking to give you strength and support. Christ has promised us that he is with us until the end of the ages—always!

   *Climate Change*

Grandchild: Is climate change a hoax?

Granddaddy: No. I believe that climate change is probably the most serious crisis our world is facing today. Climate change deniers are a genuine threat to finding a solution to this problem. Pulling our country out of the Paris Climate Agreement was an abysmal mistake, and the unwillingness of many in congress to face the reality of this problem is frightening. The recent devastating flooding of the city of Houston, TX with 52 inches of rain in a couple of days is a clear example of the present danger of climate change. Most of the world scientists all agree that climate change is due mainly to human causes, and, if humanity does not react immediately, we may not be able to save our planet from global destruction. Our oceans are encroaching more of the land before them; and our rain forests are being "logged." Global warming is causing our polar ice caps to melt, and acid rain is destroying our trees, and many are rapidly disappearing; our ozone layer is being depleted; our oceans are becoming dirty and encumbered with plastic and other non-perishable items; the weather temperatures continue to rise around the world; floods and hurricanes are more violent and more frequent; our atmosphere is more polluted and people in many places are finding it harder to breathe. The list could be expanded on and on with all our serious environmental problems.

The environmental crisis is apparent on every hand. Barry Commoner, a microbiologist, admonished some years ago that the price of pollution could cost humanity its existence. If we are going to face this problem we must overcome what some historians have called our "cowboy" philosophy of life. This philosophy believes that there will always be more land, grass, water, and clean air over the next hill; so, we can use what we want because an endless abundance lies before us. However, our ecologists and scientists are now warning us that this is simply not true any longer. The unspoiled wilderness no longer exists. We are now being encouraged to view our planet as a spaceship which has a limited supply of materials to sustain life, and, if the system is not property cared for, our supply lines can become clogged and upset the delicate, essential life support systems.

As Christians, we need to acknowledge that our destructive attitude toward our planet is wrong and frankly sinful. We are to be "caretakers" of our planet and not plunders of it. We have a proper stewardship for our planet. Let's be informed by reading the writings of ecologists who have alerted us to the seriousness of this problem. We need to write our president, congressional men and women and our senators to acknowledge and confront realistically this issue. Become educated in ways you can prevent pollution; recycle items; teach, and challenge others to realize the seriousness of this ecological problem. Climate change is indeed not a hoax but a grave world-wide problem.

Attending church

Grandchild: With all we have to do, why should we go to church?

Granddaddy: Let me respond with a story. When I was pastor of one of my churches, I was in the sanctuary of the church with some boys and girls. One of the children looked up at me and asked: "Mister Pastor, what goes on in this big room?" Many are continuing to ask that question today. And from the looks of recent church attendance records, many no longer think much is happening there. But I believe the worship that happens in that big "room" is critical for our spiritual nurture. One of the central reasons for going to church is to afford yourself the opportunity to worship God. Oh, I know, people exclaim that they can worship

God any place—in the country, by a lake, at the ocean, quietly in their room, or on the golf course, or some other place. That may be possible, but I expect it is not true for many. I have found that a designated place, like a church, affords me the time and particular place to offer my worship to God.

Remember, worship is not something God does for us; it is something we do for God. Worship gives us the occasion to acknowledge our thanksgiving for all God's blessings, offer our adoration to God, confess our sins, sense God's forgiving love and grace, and seek to find direction for our daily living. To me, worship is as essential as air is for breathing, light is for seeing, sound is for hearing, water for quenching our thirst, and food is for the nourishment of our body. My life is not the same without it.

The church also is a place where we find spiritual nurture and spiritual guidance. We are also strengthened by the support, love, and fellowship of our other Christian brothers and sisters in the faith. They also give us sustenance and courage in times of trouble, grief, failure, and other low moments. The church is the place where we are equipped to serve Christ, minister to the needy, trained to share the Gospel with others, offer our gifts to help others, and find the most meaningful ways to follow Christ. Too many today have lost their sense of the significance of the church. I believe Jesus established the church to be his vehicle to minister in the world and fortify his disciples in worship and service. I'm not giving up on the church today, but I am seeking to follow Christ as he continues his ministry through the local church. I encourage you to find a church where you can worship and serve Christ.

Jesus' Death

Grandchild: If Jesus was the Son of God, why did he let himself be killed and humiliated?

Granddaddy: Now that is a question that has resounded for centuries. The New Testament scholar, Frank Stagg, used to remind us that Jesus' death was a life taken and a life given. The death of Jesus was a life that was rejected by the religious and political leaders, betrayed by his disciples, and murdered by the Roman government. He was condemned to death by the scribes and Pharisees who thought he was a false Messiah and was a threat to their Jewish tradition and way of religion. They brought Jesus before the Roman authorities, who ruled Palestine then, and Pilate instructed that Jesus be scourged and crucified. Remember that Jesus was fully human like you and I are. In the first chapter, the Gospel of John declares boldly that "the Word that was with God and was God… and the Word became flesh and lived among us,,," as a real human being. In this sense, he was put to death by those who saw him as a threat to their way of life.

On the other side, Jesus's death was a life given. In Mark's Gospel Jesus declared that "The Son of Man also came not to be ministered unto, but to minister, and to give his life a ransom for many" (10:45). In John's Gospel, Jesus declared: "I am the good Shepherd: the good Shepherd lays down his life for the sheep (10:11). Jesus had heralded that the Kingdom of God was at hand. If the people had responded to his teachings, then, hopefully, the Kingdom reign could have begun. His death was sacrificial and self-denying in an absolute trust in God his Father's ultimate will. Many Old Testament prophets, like recorded in Isaiah 53, proclaimed that the Messiah would be rejected and crucified. Jesus bore his humiliation and death as a faithful acceptance of God's will for his life. Man/woman, the sinner, crucified the Son of Man/God's Son, who was without sin, as the Liberator—Redeemer for sinful humanity. Whole books have been written attempting to explain why Jesus died and what his death means. Without question the cross is the central symbol of Christianity. But it is more than a symbol; it represents the action, power, and love of God. Paul was bold to write: "God was in Christ reconciling the world unto himself" (2 Corinthians 5:19). He also asserted that he would preach only "Christ crucified" (1 Corinthians 2:2). What does all this mean?

The New Testament is filled with many images which the various writers employ to depict the power of God which was revealed in the cross of Christ. Paul used the image of justification which he took from the law courts. He drew pictures of redemption and emancipation from the slave market, reconciliation from the image of friendship, adoption from family life, propitiation, or ransom from the sacrificial system of Judaism, sanctification from their worship practices, and the view of setting person's account right from the accounting system. Many theologians have built their theological system around one of these pictures.

But the New Testament does not give just one interpretation of Christ's death on the cross. There are many. A casual glimpse into the New Testament discloses images of Christ's death as sacrifice, substitution, metaphors drawn from the law courts, expiation, forensic, satisfaction, example, revelation, deliverer, representative, suffering servant, lamb, and many others.

No single one of these images contains all the truth about what God has done in Christ's death. All of these images underscore the great mystery involved in the God who has loved and redeemed us on the cross. The cross can never be reduced to images of legal, judicial, transferring of guilt, paying off a debt, contracts with the devil, appeasing an angry God, etc. All of these images are just illustrations of the power and mystery of what God has done in Christ on the cross. No one of these pictures can contain the whole of the mystery. We must also affirm that God did not suddenly become loving and redeeming at the historical cross of Jesus, but the cross of Jesus reveals, I believe, the eternal nature of God's love. John wrote in Revelation about "the Lamb that was slain from the foundation of the world" (Revelation 13:8). Jesus did not die because God was angry with us and wanted to punish someone to be appeased. The cross of Jesus is the objectification into time of the eternal nature of a caring, suffering, and loving God. Jesus' humiliation and death are central to our understanding the mystery and depth of God's unconditional love for all humanity.

Resurrection of Jesus

Grandchild: The church teaches that the resurrection of Jesus was a fulfilment of the crucifixion. Is that really true?

Granddaddy: Paul claims that the church is not a memorial society but is built on the resurrection of Christ. The resurrection is the solid foundation of the Christian Church. In his Corinthian letter (1 Corinthians 15:1-11), Paul lists six resurrection appearances of Christ. There are only ten or eleven recorded in the Gospels, Acts, and Paul's letters. Paul affirms that Jesus first appeared to Peter, then to the twelve, to more than five hundred persons at one time, James, to all the apostles with Thomas present, and finally he appeared to him. The gospels state that Jesus first appeared to three women, among them Mary (Mark 16:9; Matthew 28:1-10; John 20:11-18). Paul may not have included women on his list because people might discount the experiences of women in his day. The second recorded appearance of Christ occurred on Easter afternoon as two disciples of Jesus were on their way to Emmaus (Mark 16:12-13; Luke 24:13-35). He appeared also to the disciples by the Sea of Tiberius (John 21:7-14), on a mountain in Galilee (Matthew 28:16-20), and on Mt. Olivet just before his ascension (Luke 24:50). In the Book of Acts, Luke states that Jesus "presented himself alive after his passion by many proofs, appearing to them during forty days, and speaking of the kingdom of God" (Acts 1:3).

Paul argues first that if one does not believe that Christ has been raised, our preaching is in vain. The resurrection of Christ was the foundation on which the early disciples had based their preaching. The resurrection had been the transforming factor in the faith of the early disciples. If Christ were not raised, their preaching was based on a lie, and they had no right to preach such a delusion. But Christ has been raised from the dead, Paul exclaims, and our preaching bears testimony to that reality. Continuing his argument, Paul declares that if Christ has not been raised, then your faith is in vain. If you do not believe Jesus has been raised from the grave, your faith is empty, futile, and hopeless. Instead of standing on a rock, you are positioned on quicksand. There is no solid foundation. Without the resurrection, everything in our belief tumbles but Christ has been raised; therefore, our trust is assured.

Paul went even further. "If Christ has not been raised, then we misrepresent God." In their preaching Paul and the other Christians had declared that God was like Jesus—caring, loving, suffering, redemptive, and sacrificial. The resurrection was seen as an act of God vindicating the life and ministry of Jesus. If God did not raise Jesus Christ from the grave, then the early Church misrepresented God. They have lied about God's actions. If Christ has not been raised, Paul continues to argue, we are still in our sins. Paul and others had preached that the death of Christ on the cross brings redemption, ransom, and forgiveness. The death of Christ would have been futile without the resurrection. If Christ were not raised, we are still burdened with our sins. "If Christ has not been raised," Paul continues, "then those who have died, have died hopeless, and without any possibility of life after death." If Christ has not been raised, there is no hope for any of us. Our hope in life after death is based on the assurance of his resurrection. This is the great affirmation of the Christian faith—because Christ lives we, too, shall live.

On Easter Sunday morning two thousand years later, we join the voices of millions of other Christians around the world and exclaim: "Hallelujah. Christ is risen!" With Paul, we affirm that the resurrection of Christ is the foundation of the Christian Church. It was the one thing—the only thing—that could have turned the defeated, despairing disciples into crusading evangelists for the gospel of Christ.

Death and life after death

Grandchild: Do you fear death?

Granddaddy: Well, that's not an easy question to answer. At this stage, I am not looking forward to dying. If I were in some really bad physical shape, that might afford another response. Suffering is not something anyone desires, and sometimes death is a release from suffering and pain. In that predicament, I likely would have another perspective. At this stage in life, I still have much I want to do and long to see you, my grandchildren, grow and what you will accomplish in your lives. I know death is a reality for all of us, and I hope I will not fear it when my time comes. I strive to prepare myself for this occurrence through personal, private devotions, worship, reading, and communion with God. Whether anyone is ever really prepared for death's arrival, I wonder. Death's arrival, I suppose, is our greatest occasion for faith and trust in the goodness and love of God and in the assurance of life beyond death. It is a faith adventure and not a journey with clearly prescribed luggage. I have stood by the beds of several people when they approached this final venture and watched them place their trust in the God they had loved and trusted in this life. I think that is what we all will have to do. I pray for the faith and trust to make that step into the life beyond assured that I will not travel that path alone.

Grandchild: Can we know if there is life beyond death or time for us after we die in another dimension?

Granddaddy: Many methods have been used to try to peer behind the veil of death to see if anything is there. Some have attempted to read the stars, tea leaves. crystal balls, and cards; others have listened to mediums who allegedly talk with the dead; some have even dreamed of "time machines" which would carry a person into the future and beyond. Few have found much lasting satisfaction through these paths. For many, life seems to be heading for a dead-end street. The grave seems to pronounce a final word of defeat to the meaning and purpose of life.

The New Testament, however, is bold to assert that the decisive victory over sin and death has already been won through the life, death, and resurrection of Jesus Christ. The day has come! The war may continue for some time yet, but the decisive battle has already been accomplished through Christ's victory over the grave. The last book in the Bible relates the words of victory as the seer of Patmos records his vision of the living Christ. "Behold, I am alive for evermore. Amen; and have the keys of hell and of death" (Revelation 1:18). The words of Jesus to Martha express the Christian hope: "I am the resurrection, and the life: he that believes in me, though he were dead, yet shall he live: and whosoever lives and believes in me shall never die" (John 11:25-26). The resurrection of Christ was the central thrust of the early church's preaching (Acts 4:33; 17:2 18:32; 24:15; 1 Corinthians 15:14-20; Ephesians 1:18-21; Philippians 3:10; Hebrews 13:20).

The resurrection of Jesus Christ marks the coming of the new age. Even before his death Jesus had declared that God "is not the God of the dead, but the God of the living" (Mark 12:27). And now the church proclaims that through Christ's death and resurrection forgiveness of sin and new life are available to persons of faith (Acts 5:30-31; Romans 4:25). The message, however, is that the new life is a present possession of the believer which begins with one's trust (John17:3; 2 Corinthians 4:10-11; 1 John 4:9). The Gospel of John does not make a distinction between the time of this world and the time of the realm where one lives after death. In fact, that Gospel states that eternal life is a present possession of the Christian.

Eternal life is something that transforms the present; it is a kind of existence which makes one aware of living " in eternity now. "This is life eternal, that they might know thee the only true God, and Jesus Christ, whom thou hast sent" (John 17:3). See also John 8:51-52; 11:26; Hebrews 5:6; 8:17-21. Through Christ the time barrier has been overcome.

To know God through his Son is to possess eternal life. The Greek word for eternal is not concerned so much with length of life but with quality. Eternal life is the life of God. and through an intimate, personal relationship, which Christ has made available, we can participate here and now in the eternal life of God. God's time is eternity. God is the only One "from everlasting to everlasting" (Psalm 90:2); "the same yesterday, and to-day, and forever" (Hebrews 13: 8). He is the "Alpha and Omega, ... which is, ... and which is to come, the Almighty" (Revelation 1:8).

The One who has initiated the "new creation" is the One the Scriptures declare was with God "in the beginning" (John 1:1). See also Colossians 1:15-20. The Lord over time has given those of us who live in time an opportunity to share in eternity through fellowship with God. God's love has reached out to humanity before the "foundation of the world" (John 17:24; Revelation 13:8). God's eternal love is boundless. It stretches back beyond history and forward into fulfilment of time.

The late Scottish theologian, John Baillie, told the story of a doctor who was asked by a dying man, "What do you think it will be like on the other side?" At that moment, there was heard a scratching noise at the door. "Do you hear that noise?" the doctor asked. "It is my dog who has never been in this room. He has no idea what it is like, but he knows I am here. So, it will be with the future life. We believe our Master will be there and we will be with him. That is all we need to know." I think this story conveys something about our hope for eternal life.

Loved ones watching over us

Grandchild: Are our loved ones and people we know watching over us all the time like God does, or do they just come to watch over us at certain times?

Granddaddy: There are certain persons, like spiritualists and mediums, who believe that the living can contact the dead. Persons like Edgar Cayce, Jess Stearn, James Van Praagh and Leslie Weatherhead, the English minister from the last century, and others, believe that it is possible to commune with the dead. A book, written several years ago by Van Praagh, *Talking to Heaven: A Medium's Message of Life and Death* (New York: Penguin Putnam, Inc., 1999), set forth in detail the author's claim to have communicated with the dead. In the Old Testament, there is a story where Saul seeks out the spiritualist of Endor (I Samuel 28:8ff) to see if he can contact the dead. Some interpret Jesus' transfiguration and his conversation with Moses and Elijah to be this type of experience (Matthew 17:1-8). Unfortunately, there has been a great amount of deceit, quackery and plain nonsense espoused by these who often advocate spiritualism.

Spiritualists or mediums, like Sylvia Watanabe or Sally Morgan, a British spiritualist, who has written a book titled *My Psychic Life*, declare that they have talked with the dead. I am personally very uncomfortable with the declarations by many mediums who say they have had dead people speak to them or through them. The Old Testament has strong condemnation for those who seek out mediums. For example, check Leviticus 19:31; 20:27, Deuteronomy 18:10-13, Isaiah 8:19, and 1Timothy 4:1-2. I believe we should look to the Holy Spirit as our guide, who Jesus said would teach us all things (John 14:26). Today there is a fascination with the paranormal, ghosts and spiritualism. TV shows like *The Walking Dead*, *Crossing Over* and the series *A Haunting* on the

Discovery Channel reveal this special interest. Duke University has been involved for some years now to determine whether there is any validity to spiritualism, the psychic dimension, parapsychology, and extrasensory perception. Many remain skeptical about spiritualism and dismiss it.

Some use the reference in Hebrew 12:1-2 where the writer says, "Therefore, since we are surrounded by so great a cloud of witnesses, let us also lay aside every weight and the sin that clings so closely, and let us run with perseverance that race that is set before us, looking to Jesus the pioneer and perfecter of our faith." They see this "cloud of witnesses" as the dead looking down on the living. I think this is an incorrect interpretation of the text. The author is referring to the **witness** of the "faithfulness" of those mentioned in Chapter 11, like Abel, Enoch, Noah, Abraham, Moses, David, and others in Jewish history, and not to a literal group of people sitting in a stadium watching us run in the race of life. I personally do not believe that our loved ones or others are "watching" over us. Death brings a "chasm" that cannot, I think, be traversed from the spiritual world to our physical world. Others obviously disagree with me on this.

Grandchild: Do people we know who have passed on speak to us directly or through others as well?

Granddaddy: Many find evidence for this in dreams or visions they have had of deceased loved ones. I have heard and read many stories of persons who actually make such claims. John Killinger, a minister friend and theologian, has relayed dreams about seeing his parents after they had died, and he also shared a vision a woman in Los Angeles had about her mother who had been dead more than thirty years.

This woman saw a circle of light in her hallway about fifteen inches in diameter near the baseboard ten or twelve feet ahead of her. The extremely bright light was divided equally into three segments, one gold, one rose, and the third, bluish green. In the middle of the light, stood her mother dressed in a black dress she made when she was 60 years old. In the circle of light her mother looked 60, not 87, as she was when she died. Her mother looked directly at her daughter, seriously and thoughtfully. The vision lasted, she said, several seconds.

Several years ago, I telephoned a medical doctor friend in another state whose mother had died. His mother had lived to be 85 years old. She was a committed Christian, an active church member in the church where I had been her pastor, and was always youthful, energetic, and doing for others. Several days before she died, she told her grandson that she had a dream and saw her mother who said to her, "Irene, it's time to come home."

I don't know about you, but I cannot dismiss the many experiences which people have had. It may not be scientific evidence for life beyond the grave, but it is a reassuring pointer. The Bible is filled with stories about God, angels and others communicating to persons through dreams. Can it not be possible that our loves ones can? I personally have not had any kind of experience where I have had a dream or any other awareness that a loved one, who was dead, was trying to speak to me.

Grandchild: Does God speak to us through other people, and, if so, how do we know when?

Granddaddy: I don't think God is going to "literally speak" through others to us, but God's inspiration of them might be a way of using them to share insights and spiritual guidance for us. Through their own spiritual learning and spiritual growth, God might inspire our parents, grandparents, brothers and sisters, teachers, ministers, coaches, friends, if we are married, our spouses, and many others to help us grow spiritually. When others try to guide us morally and spiritually through life, the yardstick for measuring the validity of their advice to me is "Does it conform with the teachings of Jesus and his call to follow the sacrificial way of service?" If someone is offering guidance that is immoral unethical and selfish, I know it cannot be coming from God.

Remember the story of Lazarus and the rich man in hell who asks Abraham if someone can warn his brothers here on earth so they would change. "They have Moses and the prophets; let them hear them. No, father Abraham, if one went to them from the dead, they will repent." But Abraham replies, "If they hear not Moses and the prophets, neither will they be persuaded, though one rose from the dead" (Luke 16:29-31). Persons should not be persuaded by someone claiming to talk with the dead, if what they say one should do, violates the teachings and way of life Jesus taught us. Jesus' declared in this story that people would not be persuaded by one who rose from the grave. We should not be so quick to listen to those who claim that God speaks directly to them or they hear God's voice talking to them through the "dead" with exact "instructions" for them.

Atheists and death

Grandchild: What happens to the people who don't believe in God, and, who are atheists, when they die?

Granddaddy: I believe we begin in the next life spiritually where we leave off in this physical life. Some people through their deep faith in God will be further down the spiritual trail than others who have not responded to God in this life. Atheists, who do not believe in God, will, I believe, be surprised to encounter God's presence. Their rejection of God will mean for them a "descent" into hell. This experience, I do not believe, is to punish or torment them for not believing in God, but rather is a time of teaching and learning the spiritual lessons they missed in the physical life.

If a person chose not to respond to God's love in this life, God granted that person that freedom. This has now led to their feelings of isolation and despair in the next life. I think the theologian, Nels Ferré, is possibly correct when he states that we must "preach hell as having a school and a door in it?" That means that hell may be educational and remedial, a place where we can learn and still respond to God? Some feel that this is in keeping with the one who came "to seek and to save the lost" (Luke 19:10) and who proclaimed, "if I be lifted up, I will draw all persons to me" (John 12:32). God's universal love would be defeated, I think, if an individual, even in hell, could continue to reject God's love. God would grant them that freedom, as God did in this life. But I do not believe that anyone can continuously resist God's unconditional love. That love and grace over time will eventually win that person to respond favorably to God.

When a person knows his or her needs in this earthly life, he or she is going to seek to go into God's kingdom beyond death to the level where they can continue to grow and develop deeper in their relationship to Christ. Some are on a higher plain spiritually than others when they die. Some are so low spiritually that for them, this is Hell. They are far from God. This would be an atheist. There are others, even Christians, saved by grace, who will be spiritually on different plateaus. We are not going to know where anybody else is, I don't believe. It's like each one of us has a spiritual cup. I know how much is in my cup, but I don't know how much spiritual life is in your cup. Frankly, I know that is not my concern, unless I am a teacher who is going to help others move further along the spiritual plain. I don't think that even, when we arrive in the heavenly realm, that we are full-grown Christians. I think we will have eternity to keep growing and seeking to be more like God.

 *Other world religions*

Grandchild: Will people of other religions who have never heard or responded to Jesus be doomed to hell?

Granddaddy: There are many who believe that is true. They like to quote the scriptures that say: "No one comes to the father but by me" or "whosoever believes on the name of Jesus will be saved." I think we are charged to share the good news about God's love in Christ with others. But, if a person has never heard of Christ, how can he or she respond? The failure seems to me with us not them. I like what John Baillie, the Scottish theologian, said. "Whenever a person has responded to the highest revelation he has about God, he has responded to the Eternal Christ." Jesus also said, "I have other sheep that do not belong to this fold. I must bring them also, and they will listen to my voice. So, there will be one flock, one shepherd" (John 10:16). The same God, who loves us through Jesus Christ, is working through the other religions of the world to bring men and women into God's universal grace and unconditional love. When we enter the next adventure of life after death, we will be surprised at the wideness and depth of God's eternal love--"like the wideness of the sea," as the hymn writer suggests.

In Revelation 21:25, it states that there will be no closed gates in Heaven. Gates are located on the east, north, south, and west, indicating that persons can enter by many roadways into the presence of God. The gates will never be shut by day or night. This affirms that there is not just one way to God. Jesus stands at the doorway of the human heart and knocks inviting anyone to respond. The doors of heaven are open to all who will enter. According to John, all barriers in Heaven have been removed by God's love, grace, and mercy. God's presence and the depth of God's love fill the New Jerusalem, and everyone there can commune with God.

 *Knowing each other in heaven*

Grandchild: Will we know our family and others in Heaven?

Granddaddy: I believe that we will know each other in Heaven. If we do not have memory of each other, what kind of happiness would that bring? Memory is a distinct part of our being a person. We all know what it is like to be with a loved one who has dementia, or Alzheimer's. We know them, and they do not know us. It's sad. That would not be heaven.

Some have asked, "If we can remember, will that not cause us pain, hurt and other negative feelings?" Some of those feelings may be there, and maybe that's why we need our heavenly school to guide us through them to a stage to handle those feelings properly.

We can take comfort and reassurance in Jesus' words to the thief on the cross. "Today, you will be with me in paradise" (Luke 23:43). If they did not recognize one another, why would they want to meet again? In the transfiguration, Jesus knows Elijah and Moses (Matthew 17:3). Paul says, "we will know as we have been known" (1 Corinthians 13:12). Jesus did tell us that there would be no marriage in Heaven, but we would be like the angels. That does not mean we would not know nor love our spouse or other loved ones.

Those missed the most

Grandchild: Of all the people who had an influence on your life and are now dead, who do you miss the most?

Granddaddy: I suppose my answer to the question would be my parents and your grandmother's parents. I think we do not re- alize how much impact our parents have upon us until they are no longer here. They set me on the proper paths of honesty, hard work, self-discipline, to do my best, respect, the importance of church and worship, the importance of family, moral values, endurance, good manners, self-reliance, and, frankly, most of the values I prize the most. Your grandmother's parents likewise had a deep impact on my life, especially after Emily and I got married. I miss the opportunity to dialogue with Mr. Campbell about many matters, especially financial issues or how to repair something. Neither set of these parents was perfect, but their influence for good is life-last- ing. I regret that I did not express my appreciation for what they meant to me more fully. Now, it's too late. I wish they could see their great-grandchildren and what you have achieved in your lives so far. I know they would be proud.

Jesus as a Jew and us

Grandchild: If Jesus was Jewish, why aren't Christians Jewish, and why do most Jews not believe in Jesus?

Granddaddy: Jesus was indeed a Jew and all of his disciples were also Jewish, including the Apostle Paul. Jesus began his ministry in Palestine, a Jewish nation, where he was born and where he grew up. Most of his early followers were Jewish, with a few exceptions like a Roman centurion whose child Jesus healed, a Samaritan woman, etc. The Apostle Paul had a dream/vision in which he heard a "call" to preach the Gospel to the Gentiles (Acts 16:6-10). Gentiles are all of those who are not Jews, regardless of the country. Under Paul's preaching and teaching, Gentiles begin to believe in Jesus and became his followers, and the early churches came into exitance. You and I as Americans, and Christians in other Gentile countries, are Christians because of our belief in Jesus Christ as Lord, but we are not Jewish. Jews are a race of people who trace their descent from the Israelites of the Bible and practice the religion of Judaism. Today Jews live in many parts of the world, including the United States, and have their own worship and synagogues.

Most Jews have not accepted Jesus as their savior, because they do not believe he was the Messiah that was prophesied in the Old Testament. They are still looking for the coming of that Messiah. They do not believe that the Messiah would be crucified. For them that is a big stumbling block, as Paul wrote about in some of his letters (1 Corinthians 1:23). Many Jews see Jesus as a great Jewish teacher or prophet but not the long-awaited Messiah. The disciples of Jesus and Paul believed that Jesus was indeed the promised Messiah who became our Redeemer and Lord. The death of Jesus on the cross and his resurrection are paramount to our Christian understanding of who the Messiah really was. The fact that the early Christians changed their day of worship from the Jewish Sabbath to Sunday is a strong affirmation of the resurrection of Jesus on Sunday, the first day of the week. This was a bold declaration in their assurance of the risen Christ and the awareness that salvation in Jesus was not limited to Jews but to all who would believe.

The second coming

Grandchild: What do you think Jesus would say if he came back today to our modern world? What would he do?

Granddaddy: If Jesus came to our world today as he came 2000 years ago to Palestine, I think he would be disappointed to see that wars, bigotry, prejudice, hatred, racism, poverty, diseases were still so rampant in our world in spite of the Christian Gospel that had been around for all these years. I think he would be disappointed that the church focuses too much on its own survival and self-absorption than ministering effectively to the needs all around it. He would be disappointed that the great Christian virtues of faith, hope, and love were not more visible in every Christian's life. He would be disappointed that Christians had not really heard or practiced the commandments to love our neighbors as ourselves and likewise our enemies. He would be disappointed that we had too often made the church a place of wealth, power, and dogmatism rather than a place of acceptance, sacrificial ministry, grace, and love. The list could go on.

I think he would be encouraged by the groups and churches that engaged in peace efforts, those striving to overcome racism and hatred, those working to assist the hungry, ill, poor and needy in the world, those going to needy places to bring education, agricultural training, and medical assistance, those sharing the light of the Gospel in dark corners of our country and around the world, those genuinely trying to find ways to cross bridges to show love and respect for their brothers and sisters of many races and colors.

He would be pleased by any small effort that was undertaken to try and share the message of God's unconditional love.

What would Jesus do? I think he would seek to help guide and equip his followers in how best to share and minister God's sacrificial love in our world today. As he did 2000 years ago, his method would be by word and deed, teaching and healing, accepting and loving, forgiving and challenging, witnessing and sacrificing. He would not try to coerce us in his ways, but summon us to follow him in love and service. As always, he would give us the freedom to follow him or not. His way, I believe, would be more loving than judgmental, more encouraging than scornful, more gracious than hateful, more receptive than prejudicial, more caring than vindictive, and above all more willing to guide us in the sacrificial way he has called us to follow.

Grandchild: Will Jesus come back to earth?

Granddaddy: Yes. I believe he will. The New Testament is filled with references that this will happen. Luke 21:27 says, "And they will see the son of man coming in a cloud with power and great glory." In John 14:2, Jesus said, "I have gone to prepare a place for you and after that I will come again and receive you unto myself." In Acts 1:11, we read, "this Jesus who was taken up from you into heaven will come in the same way as you saw him go into heaven." Paul in almost all of his writings, except maybe Galatians, Ephesians, and Philemon, speaks about the coming of Christ. At first Paul wrote in a sense of expecting an immediate return. Later, I think, he begins to change his view. Even as we observe the Lord's Supper, Paul has reminded us that "we do this until the Lord comes," (1 Corinthians 11:26). James suggested the coming of Christ was near at hand" (James 5:8). Revelation is filled with all kinds of apocalyptic symbols, especially in Chapters 19, 20 and 21.

Many like to refer to this belief as the Second Coming. The words, "Second Coming," however, do not appear in the New Testament. The closest you can find similar wording anywhere is in Hebrews 9:28, "He shall appear a second time, apart from sin, to those awaiting him unto salvation." The earliest use of the term comes about the middle of the second century. The New Testament term in Greek is "*Parousia*" which means "presence" or "coming." There are a variety of views on how this concept is to be understood. A popular position is called the *postmillennialist* view. These advocates believe that a sign that the end is near was realized in the return of Israel to the Holy Land. They believe that the world is improving, and that Christ will remain in heaven and work through his church to redeem the world. At the end of a thousand years, Christ will come and intervene in the world and bring history to its conclusion.

Another view is the *premillennialist* interpretation. These persons take the opposite view of the *postmillennialists,* instead of the world getting better they believe that it is becoming more evil. For them too, the return of Israel to its home land was a sign of the end. The rapture is going to take the saints out of this world. After seven years of tribulation, there will be a thousand-year reign of Christ, and then the judgment will come. There are four resurrections and five judgments in this theory. It is very complicated. They have developed charts and graphs to help people understand their beliefs. This is the interpretation that the popular but distorted novel series, *Left Behind* by Tim LaHaye, is based upon. Another interpretation is called the *amillennialist* view. To them the thousand-year reign is just symbolic. Christ began reigning on the cross, and he is continuing to reign and will reign until the end of history. There are, of course, several other interpretations of the "Second Coming."

How do we understand the concept of *parousia* or the Second Coming? Let me state first that I do not believe, that we can speak of a future coming in a way that denies the presence of Christ today. We do not follow an absent Lord. Our Lord is not away some place, apart from us. Jesus said, "Lo, I am with you always" (Matthew 28:20). "I have come that you might have life and have it more abundantly" (John 10:10). "I stand at the door and knock, and if anyone will open, I will come in and sup with him" (Revelation 3:20). "For me to live is Christ," (Philippians 1:20), Paul says. "The word became flesh and dwelt among us" (John 1:14) --the Incarnation. "You abide in me," Jesus said, "and I in you" (John 15:4). John 14 reminds us that Jesus "will come again and receive us unto himself" (John 14:3).

I believe that when one individual comes to Jesus Christ, he or she opens his or her life to Christ, and Jesus comes into that life. That is Jesus' coming to them. After that coming, we seek to follow Jesus. When we die and step into eternity, Jesus comes into our lives in a new way. He brings judgment, yes, but there is judgment with love, grace, and his presence. What is referred to as the *final* "Second Coming," I believe, will be when Jesus comes in his fullness to establish his reign of peace, justice, and righteousness. It will be the fulfilment of the Kingdom of God on earth. And I believe only God knows what that will be like, and when it will happen.

Changes in Christianity

Grandchild: Do you believe Christianity and religion itself has changed since Jesus was on earth? How much has it changed?

Granddaddy: Well, yes, there have been many changes. When Jesus ascended into Heaven, he left the charge to his disciples to preach the Gospel in all the world. The Christian church started in a small way with a handful of believers under the early disciples and then spread to the Gentile world through the preaching of the Apostle Paul. Today there are millions of believers and churches around the world of every race and nationality. The early Christians were often poor and met in homes, caves or wherever they could find a location. Today there are many splendid institutional wealthy churches, and many individual Christians with wealth. Many more world religions are known today than in the time of Jesus. Many of them like Buddhism and Hinduism were in existence but unknown to the Jews in Palestine. Now Christianity has to seek to understand them and relate to them.

There is no question that Jesus established the church or community of believers, but I'm not certain he envisioned it becoming established institutions that "fight" each other for members, territory, and material goods. I have difficulty in believing he envisioned the "priestly" hierarchy that has been created in the many denominations today. The body of believers were to love, nurture, support, care for one another, especially the poor, bear one another's burdens, worship together, share the Gospel with others, and live out the serving ministry like Jesus taught his disciples to follow. Some of our churches do this in a small way but far from what, I think, Jesus would have us do. I honestly reflect often on how I wonder Jesus might appraise the churches today and the way we minister in his name. And that is coming from one who has spent his life in church-related work as a minister and a seminary professor.

A Follower of Jesus

Grandchild: What does it mean to be a follower of Jesus Christ?

Granddaddy: When we turn to the New Testament, we find that Christians are called to follow Jesus Christ. In at least eighty-seven references, the four Gospels denote Jesus saying to those who would become his disciples: "Follow me." His followers are called to be disciples-learners, called to be saints, called into fellowship of God's son, Jesus Christ, our Lord, called out of darkness, called to eternal life, called to liberty, and called according to his purpose. We are called to be possessed by Christ, who is Lord of all of life. The early Christians were called men and women of The Way. That Way was the Christ-like—way of love and service, modeled after our Lord himself.

When a person makes a commitment of faith in Jesus Christ as Lord and Savior, that person is declaring that he or she wants to follow in the pathway of the life and teachings of Jesus. But many other voices from many quarters are screaming at us to follow their lead.

We hear/see/feel them calling us to follow them down the paths of materialism, pleasure, the "Playboy" philosophy of life, financial security, sexual gratification, comfort, apathy, political loyalty, religious absolutism, bigotry, racism, modernism, and countless others. How do we discern the distinguishable voice of Christ from the illegitimate ones?

Even in the realm of religion many voices cry out to us to follow them. How do we determine Christ's real voice from the false ones? There so many religious voices from around the world with so many valuable insights and beliefs in all of them. Likewise, the Christian voices are mixed with fundamental certainty to agnostic Christianity, biblical literalism and inerrancy to prosperity gospel, the only true church to come as you are and leave as you came invitations, narrow-minded belief to anything goes philosophy, or an eternal quest for the truth with an openness to a growing faith. Many in our world today have turned a deaf ear to religion altogether and declare "none" as their faith perspective. They are weary with the summons to believe based on dogma, a religious book, church affiliation, the "final answers," or any narrow view of "spirituality." So, what do we do?

I believe that the summons to follow Christ means that He is our standard, model, goal, example, director, and supporter. We follow him in our example of the necessity of worship, spiritual growth, service, and love. This means we know we will never arrive fully grown or complete with spiritual knowledge as we follow Christ. We strive always to be open and growing in our faith and awareness; acknowledging our sins and inadequacies; alert to our need for spiritual and mental discipline; relentless in our pursuit of integrity; always reaching for the highest and best we can be in the challenging adventure of following in the Way of Jesus Christ. Whatever direction you seek to take in your daily living, I believe, you should strive to follow in the Christ-like sacrificial way of service and seeking to love God with all your being and your neighbor as yourself.

Getting old

Grandchild: What is it like to get old?

Granddaddy: Ha! That's a good question. When I became 80, I told my brother, Preston, that I always thought 80 was old until I became 80. "Billy," Preston responded. "80 is old!" And he is right, of course. But it is hard for me to think that I am now old. But at 83, I'll have to admit that I am indeed old. But in many ways, I do not feel or think old. I realize that physically I no longer have the strength that I once had, and I do get tired quicker, and it takes longer to get over a long day's work in the yard. I also have more aches and pains than I used to have. But I am still in good physical shape for my age, and I continue to exercise by walking each morning, going to the YMCA several days a week, swimming laps in the pool, and doing yard work.

Even in old age, if we take care of ourselves, life can still be good and meaningful. I now take medication for type two diabetes that I did not have to take when I was younger, but my diabetes is until control and gives me no serious problems. I am fortunate that I do not have to take any other medications. Getting older has its pluses too. I know much more about life and its joys and struggles than I did when I was young. With old age, much wisdom has been acquired, and this enables me to have deeper insights into problems and issues today. Material things are not as important, and I can focus more on spiritual matters and relationships. Old age forces you to get your priorities in order, to build closer relationships with family and friends, because no one knows how long one may live. If we remain healthy and mentally alert, growing older can be a good experience and not a negative or dreaded one. One of the saddest things about getting old is seeing many of your close friends become ill, or get dementia, or go into nursing homes, or die. It causes one to try and take advantage of one's friendships and enjoy life with family and friends as long as you can.

Retirement

Grandchild: What is retirement like?

Granddaddy: Some people dread retirement, but I have found it an exciting new chapter in my life. I confess that I do enjoy the leisure time it affords in the morning to read the paper, listen to the news, drink my coffee, and not have to rush off to work. It has also given me more opportunities to travel and visit places I had wanted to see. I have found opportunities to serve as interim pastor in various churches in different states, give lectures to pastor's conferences and retreats, write books that I did not have time to do earlier, and more time to do yard work and other chores.

I think retirement has been a good chapter in my life, because I prepared for it by putting money in my retirement funds early in life. And this has enabled us not to struggle financially as some must do. I would encourage you to begin early in your life putting aside at least 10 percent of your income into retirement funds. Get a good financial advisor to assist you with this. Good health has also made a big difference for your grandmother and me. We try to exercise and eat well. Do that and for goodness sake don't smoke. Retirement offers more time to do some of the things we did not have time to do when we were working. We try to stay active with our exercises, reading, traveling, church worship and ministries, time with family and friends.

Most difficult experiences

Grandchild: What has been the most difficult experience you have had to face in life?

Granddaddy: To be honest, it is not easy to select only one experience, but, if I must make a choice, I would say learning how to respond graciously to people in churches where I have served as pastor who have been very critical and even abusive in their attitude toward me. We all want to be accepted and loved and appreciated by others, but sometimes that does not happen. Reacting in a Christian and noncombative manner was not always easy, especially if they seemed to be threatening my job as pastor. I did not experience this much in my ministry, but in one of my churches, it was an experience that I had to endure for a lengthy period.

Writing

Grandchild: You have written a number of books. Do you think you have a handle on how to write today?

Granddaddy: I don't know if anyone who writes can say that he or she has a "handle" on how to write. I certainly would not say that I have a handle on it. I feel I am always still learning how to do research, think through a project, how to express my thoughts clearly and creatively, and what way will best expound whatever I am presently writing. In some way, every new writing project is indeed unique.

Years ago, I used to do my writing by hand and had to get someone else to type it for me. Today I do my writing on the computer which enables me to add, change, insert, or move at a pace I can direct. Ideally, I prefer to write in the mornings but often, if an idea comes, I will insert it whenever that occurs any time in the day or night. Sometimes in the past, with deadlines on material for articles, I have stayed up all night writing. I don't do that now. Presently I am working on several books— ***A Handbook on Pastoral Prayers***; and ***Lessons from Old Testament Characters*** and on some other not yet clearly defined projects. I will work on one or the other at different times when I am moved to focus on that particular book. Sometimes I may stay with one for a good part of the day or only for a few minutes.

I try to do long range planning and wide reading. Trying to complete or start a writing project at the last minute or preparing a sermon on Saturday night will cause sermon or writing block. I always project writing projects to do down the road, like I'm thinking about books on the "parables of Jesus," "Old Testament characters," 'a series on the psalms," etc. I gather material, thoughts, and do reading and research in those areas. I take breaks to do family things, exercise, yard work, travel, watch ball games, take trips, do interim ministries, teach some, etc. I can't imagine being bored or burned out. I do not think I will live long enough to do all the projects I really want to do.

Questions From a Four- and Eight-Year-Old Grandchild

Grandchild: If God created the earth, who created the universe?

Granddaddy: In the first book in the Bible, Genesis 1:1-2, it reads, "In the beginning when God created the heavens and the earth, the earth was a formless void and darkness covered the face of the deep." God not only created our earth but the entire universe. Everything that exists has come about from God's creation.

Grandchild: How did God create people?

Granddaddy: We read in the book of Genesis 1:27 that "God created humankind in his image … male and female, he created them." In Genesis 2:7 the writer describes God's creation of man this way: "The Lord formed man from the dust of the ground, and breathed into his nostrils the breath of life; and the man became a living being." This tells us that God created people as well as the rest of the universe. All life has its origin in God's creative action.

Grandchild: How was God created?

Granddaddy: The Bible teaches us that God has no beginning or end. God has always existed. The Bible describes God as eternal in Genesis 21:33, Isaiah 40:28, and Romans 16:26. God was not created, God is the Almighty Creator. God is the Alpha and the Omega---the beginning and the end. This is the great mystery about God's existence.

Grandchild: What did God do before he created the world?

Granddaddy: That's a difficult question to know an answer for sure. I read somewhere that Pope Francis answered that question by saying that before God created the world God loved, because God is love. The Bible says that God is love, and I think God created the world and men and women because God loves us.

Grandchild: What is God like?

Granddaddy: God is like your mother and father who love you very much. God wants the very best for you. God is always with you and is watching over you in the daytime and at night while you sleep.

Grandchild: Can I talk to God?

Granddaddy: You can talk to God through prayer. You can speak to God silently in your thoughts and say to him what you want to ask or tell him.

Grandchild: How will I hear God?

Granddaddy: God will speak silently to you in your thoughts and heart. You won't hear a spoken voice. God talks silently to our heart. Sometimes God uses another person, like a mother or father or friend, to tell you what he wants you to hear.

Grandchild: Will God punish me if I have been bad?

Granddaddy: No. God does not punish us when we do something wrong. God wants to help us do the right thing. God loves us and is always trying to help us do the right thing. But he will let us decide whether we will do what is right or choose to do wrong. Even if we do something wrong, God still loves us.

Grandchild: Does God make me get sick?

Granddaddy: No. We get sick because of germs, viruses, weaknesses, or some other reason. God wants us to be well, and he loves us. God will not hurt us.

Grandchild: Every year I am getting bigger. What makes me grow?

Granddaddy: God has made us with a marvelous gene that makes us grow until we reach the point the gene has for us to stop growing. That's the wonderful way God has made us. We can't make it happen; it just does. It's the way God created us.

Grandchild: Our dog, Drexler, has gotten old. When he dies will he go to Heaven?

Granddaddy: I don't know if dogs or other pets go to Heaven or not. I know many of us will miss our beloved pets if they are not there.

Grandchild: Why did God make the sky blue?

Granddaddy: I, of course, do not know for certain. But I think God loves colors. The sky is blue, and the grass is green, and there are flowers of many colors. Look all around you at the beautiful colors in our world, especially in the fall of the year with the many colors in the leaves on the trees as they turn. Even snow, although it is white, is still beautiful. Isn't it?

Grandchild: Clouds are white, too.

Granddaddy: Yes. And aren't they beautiful, too?

Grandchild: If Mary is Jesus' mother and Jesus is God's son, does that mean that God and Mary are married?

Granddaddy: That is a much harder question than you can imagine. No. God and Mary were not married. The Gospels tell us that Mary was a young unmarried woman when the angel of the Lord told her that she was going to have God's son. In some way that we do understand, called a miracle, God's Spirit came to Mary and she became pregnant. That's what is known as the "virgin birth." Remember that God is Spirit and does not have a human body. Mary married a man named Joseph, who was the father of several other children that Mary had, but he was not the father of Jesus.

Grandchild: When it is real dark in my room when I go to bed, sometimes I'm scared. Is God there to protect me?

Granddaddy: Yes, honey. God is there to watch over you. God is always present with us, even if we don't know it or see him. God is continually awake to be near you. Sleep, trusting that God is with you.

Grandchild: Did God send the hurricane that caused all the floods in Florida recently to punish people for being bad?

Granddaddy: No. God did not send the hurricane to punish people. God is a God of love and does not do things to hurt people. Our world was created with freedom to respond to the natural laws, and sometimes these natural occurrences happen as they follow their own patterns. Floods, earthquakes, hurricanes, wild fires, and other natural disasters are not God punishing people for being bad, but natural things that happen in our world.

Grandchild: Is God white or black? I hear some say one thing and others something different.

Granddaddy: God is neither and both. What I mean by that is God is Spirit and contains all colors of people and is not confined to any one race of people or color. God made all people. No matter what color we are, God created us and loves us as his children.

Grandchild: Is God a man? We pray to God as our Father.

Granddaddy: Yes, we often pray to God as our Father, but God is not a man or a woman. Remember, God is Spirit and contains all that we know about a man and woman's nature. But God is not limited by either man or woman's nature. God is beyond what we call male or female, but can be prayed to, I think, as either Father or Mother or just as Loving God.

Grandchild: When I go to church I keep looking for God. Is there some special place I need to look to find him there?

Granddaddy: I wish I could tell you that there is a special place in church where you can see God. God cannot be seen with our visible eyes, because God is Spirit. We can only feel God in our heart or hear him in our mind. God is present, but not in human form like your mother and daddy. Sometimes in the quietness of church, you may have that "warm" feeling that lets you know that God is there. Remember, even if you can't see God in church, or any place else, God is indeed there.

Afterword

Our journey through life will always produce more questions. I want to encourage my grandchildren to be open to raise their questions and to be assured that God welcomes them as well.

CPSIA information can be obtained
at www.ICGtesting.com
Printed in the USA
LVHW111018080320
649322LV00003B/799

9 781631 996894